Pennsylvania
REAL ESTATE
EXAM
PREP

THIRD EDITION

Dearborn™
Real Estate Education

This publication is designed to provide accurate and authoritative information in regard to the subject matter covered. It is sold with the understanding that the publisher is not engaged in rendering legal, accounting, or other professional service. If legal advice or other expert assistance is required, the services of a competent professional should be sought.

President: Roy Lipner
Vice President of Product Development and Publishing: Evan M. Butterfield
Managing Editor: Kate DeVivo
Editorial Assistant: Tom Selley
Director of Production: Daniel Frey
Senior Managing Editor: Jack Kiburz
Creative Director: Lucy Jenkins
Typesetter: Leah Strauss

Published by Dearborn™ Real Estate Education
30 South Wacker Drive, Suite 2500
Chicago, Illinois 60606-7481
(312) 836-4400
www.dearbornRE.com

Printed in the United States of America

06   07   10   9   8   7   6   5   4   3   2   1

INTRODUCTION

Welcome to *Pennsylvania Real Estate Exam Prep*! When you bought this book, you showed that you were serious about passing the exam and getting your real estate license. This is *NOT* an easy test. For people whose test-taking skills are weak or who haven't adequately prepared, the exam can be a nightmare. For those who have taken the time and effort to study and review, however, the exam can be a much more positive experience.

It's pretty obvious, though, that if you practice and review key material, your test score will improve. This book is your key to exam success.

The process is simple: Begin by thoroughly reviewing whatever classroom materials and notes you have. Then, work your way through the practice questions, taking your time and answering each one carefully. Finally, check your answers by studying the Answer Key, where you'll find both the correct answer to each question as well as an explanation of *why* that answer is correct. In addition, most answers cite the specific section of either the Real Estate License and Registration Act (RELRA) or the rules and regulations of the State Real Estate Commission that directly address the question topic.

Remember: These 225 questions reflect as closely as possible the topic coverage of the state-specific portion of your exam only! For the balance of the test, you'll need to use a "national" exam prep book. And remember, too, that it takes study and hard work on your part to pass the licensing exam: no single study aid will do the trick alone.

Experts who are familiar with the Pennsylvania licensing examination as well as with real estate law and practice prepared this book. You've taken the first step toward your success as a real estate professional. Good Luck!

Dearborn™ Real Estate Education

PRACTICE QUESTIONS

1. A listing broker procures a ready, willing, and able buyer for her seller-principal. The seller first accepts the buyer's offer in writing, then experiences a change of heart and withdraws the original acceptance. In this situation, the broker

   1. may be entitled to collect a commission.
   2. has no recourse because the transaction was never completed.
   3. may sue the buyer.
   4. may retain the deposit as compensation.

2. In Pennsylvania, brokerage fees are

   1. set by law.
   2. set by the Pennsylvania Real Estate Commission.
   3. determined by local groups of brokers operating a multiple listing service.
   4. negotiable between the consumer and the broker employed by the consumer.

3. Commissions earned by a broker in a real estate sales transaction

   1. are determined by agreement of the broker and the consumer.
   2. may be shared with an unlicensed person who is employed by the broker, provided that such person aided the broker in bringing the buyer and seller together.
   3. may be deducted from the earnest money deposit and claimed by the broker as soon as the buyer and seller execute the purchase and sales agreement.
   4. are based on a schedule of commission rates set by the multiple listing service.

4. Several weeks after a closing, an associate broker received a thank-you letter and a nice bonus check from the seller of the house. The associate broker cashed the check because he felt it was earned. In this situation, which of the following is *TRUE*?

   1. The associate broker may accept the bonus because he is licensed as an associate broker.
   2. Accepting the money is allowed if more than 30 days have elapsed since closing.
   3. The associate broker may accept the money if his broker permits him to do so.
   4. Accepting the money is a violation of the License and Registration Act.

5. What determines the amount of compensation to be paid to a licensed real estate salesperson by the employing broker?

   1. Negotiation between the broker and property owner at the time property is listed for sale
   2. The rules and regulations of the multiple listing service to which the broker belongs
   3. The code of ethics of the association or board of REALTORS®
   4. The contract between the employing broker and the licensed real estate salesperson

6. A real estate company has entered into agency agreements with both a seller and a buyer. The buyer is interested in making an offer on the seller's property. Can this occur?

   1. No, because the real estate company would then be a dual agent.
   2. Yes, as long as written agency agreements have been entered into with both parties.
   3. Yes, if the seller has agreed to pay the commission.
   4. Yes, if both the buyer and seller give their informed consent in writing after receiving full disclosure regarding dual agency.

7. The listing agreement with a seller has expired, and the seller lists with a different brokerage firm. The original listing salesperson now represents a buyer interested in the seller's property. The original listing agent

   1. is a dual agent and must get permission from both parties.
   2. cannot disclose to the buyer information about terms acceptable to the seller that were received during the listing period.
   3. cannot disclose to the buyer information about the physical condition of the property.
   4. cannot represent the buyer.

8. A buyer contacts a real estate office and indicates an interest in purchasing a home in the area. In the absence of a buyer agency relationship with the buyer, a salesperson from the real estate office should do all of the following *EXCEPT*

   1. provide the buyer with information on properties for sale in the area.
   2. give the buyer information on mortgage interest rates and terms.
   3. discuss specific information regarding the buyer's motivation and urgency.
   4. explain to the buyer about buyer agency, seller agency, and dual agency.

9. In a dual agency situation, a broker may collect compensation from both the seller and the buyer if

   1. the broker is licensed as a dual agent.
   2. the buyer and the seller are related by blood or marriage.
   3. both parties give their informed consent in writing to the dual compensation.
   4. both parties are represented by attorneys.

10. A buyer is interested in seeing a house listed with XYZ Realty but does not wish to enter into an agency relationship. A salesperson from LMN Realty can show the buyer the house if

   1. XYZ Realty has obtained the seller's written consent to offer subagency, and the buyer is given a consumer notice and disclosure stating that LMN Realty represents the seller.
   2. XYZ Realty obtains LMN Realty's consent to subagency, and the buyer is given an Agency Disclosure Notice stating that XYZ Realty represents the seller.
   3. the buyer verbally agrees to a buyer relationship with LMN Realty.
   4. a salesperson from XYZ Realty accompanies them during the showing.

11. A real estate broker has signed an agency agreement with a tenant who is looking for an apartment to rent. The broker does not charge a fee to prospective tenants; rather, the broker receives compensation from landlords. The broker tells a landlord that the prospective tenant could probably pay a somewhat higher rent than the landlord is asking. In this situation, the licensee

   1. owes the fiduciary agency duties to the landlord, who pays the broker's fee.
   2. appropriately disclosed to the landlord under these circumstances.
   3. violated the fiduciary duties owed to the tenant.
   4. has no duty of confidentiality because the licensee is not charging a fee to prospective tenants.

12. A licensed salesperson obtains a listing. Several days later, the salesperson meets prospective buyers at the property and tells them, "I am the listing agent for this property, and so I'm very familiar with it." He then proceeds to engage in substantive discussion about their needs and motivations as he shows them the property. Under these circumstances, the salesperson has

1. failed to comply with state law regarding disclosure of agency relationships.
2. properly disclosed his agency relationship with the seller.
3. made a substantial misrepresentation because the listing belongs to the broker.
4. created a dual agency, which is a violation of the Pennsylvania Real Estate License and Registration Act.

13. A real estate company has entered into agency agreements with both a seller and a buyer, both of whom have signed a Dual Agency Consent Agreement. The salesperson with the realty company that has been working with the buyer may

1. provide comparable market data about recent sales to the buyer.
2. disclose the buyer's financial qualifications, motivation, and urgency to the seller.
3. disclose to the buyer that the seller will accept less than the listing price.
4. disclose to the seller that the buyer will pay more than the offering price.

14. While representing a seller under a listing contract, the broker learned confidential information about the seller's urgency to sell and minimum acceptable selling price. The listing expired, and the property was listed with a different broker. The original broker now represents a buyer client who is interested in making an offer on the property. At this time, the broker

1. as buyer's agent must disclose to the buyer any information the broker knows about the seller's motivation and minimum acceptable price.
2. must refer the buyer prospect to the new listing broker to write the offer to purchase.
3. must renounce his agency relationship with the buyer and act as the subagent of the seller.
4. may not reveal confidential information of the seller or use it to the advantage of the buyer client.

15. While negotiating terms of a listing contract with a seller, the seller suggests a listing price significantly below what the salesperson believes the property would sell for in the open market. What is the best course of action for the licensee to follow?

1. List the property at the seller's price in anticipation of a fast sale and easy commission
2. Disclose the salesperson's professional opinion of value and recommend that the property be listed at market value
3. Recommend a net listing at the seller's suggested price
4. Directly purchase the property at the seller's price without entering into a listing contract

16. Which of the following is *TRUE* regarding agency relationships between licensees and consumers?

    1. All agency relationships must be expressly created by written agreements.
    2. An open listing agreement creating an agency relationship between a seller and broker may be an oral agreement.
    3. If a broker chooses to represent both buyers and sellers under agency relationships, the broker must adopt a policy appointing designated agents.
    4. A broker may not represent both a buyer and seller as an agent in the same transaction.

17. An agent is representing the seller and working with a buyer. While reviewing terms of an agreement of sale with a buyer, how should the agent respond to the buyer's concerns about certain provisions in the agreement?

    1. Because the agent represents the seller, the agent has no obligation to respond to the buyer's concerns.
    2. The agent should advise the buyer to seek expert advice from an attorney-at-law regarding his concerns.
    3. The agent should address the concerns raised by the buyer directly and advise the buyer regarding the provisions that are of concern.
    4. The agent should recommend that the buyer contract with a buyer's agent.

18. A salesperson receives an offer on a property currently listed exclusively with another broker. The salesperson approaches the seller with the offer and a new listing contract, recommending that the seller terminate the current listing and list with his company in order to keep everything "in house." The salesperson

    1. is acting in the best interests of the sellers, who should cancel the current listing so that they can accept the offer without unnecessary complications.
    2. should have referred the buyers to the listing broker, who should have written and presented their offer.
    3. has violated the license law by inducing the seller to break the current exclusive-listing contract in order to substitute a new one, which would result in a personal gain to the salesperson.
    4. should transfer his license to the broker who has the property listed for sale in order to avoid any potential conflict.

19. A broker who operated a sole proprietorship dies. Another licensed broker is now supervising the termination of the business of the deceased broker. The second broker may

    1. take new listing agreements not to exceed a term of 90 days.
    2. promote unexpired listings unless the seller elects to cancel the agreement.
    3. not take pending agreements of sale to closing.
    4. hire new licensees.

20. The salesperson represents the seller in a transaction. When prospective buyers ask to look at the property, the salesperson must

    1. tell them that they must first enter into a buyer representation agreement with another licensee.
    2. have the buyer sign the Consumer Notice prior to showing the property.
    3. inform them that the salesperson represents the seller's interests and maintain appropriate documentation of the disclosure.
    4. Show them the property without making any disclosures about the salesperson's relationship with the seller, because such disclosure would be a violation of the salesperson's fiduciary duties.

21. A broker listed a small office building. Because the property is in excellent condition and produces a good, steady income, the broker's salesperson has decided to purchase it as an investment. If the broker's salesperson wishes to buy this property, the salesperson must

    1. resign as the broker's agent and make an offer after the owner has retained another broker.
    2. have a third party purchase the property on the salesperson's behalf so that the owner does not learn the true identity of the purchaser.
    3. obtain permission from the Pennsylvania Real Estate Commission.
    4. inform the owner in writing that the salesperson is a licensee of the listing broker when making an offer.

22. A real estate licensee must give the Consumer Notice to prospective purchasers/tenants at

    1. the initial interview.
    2. every open house they attend.
    3. the closing table.
    4. the time an offer to purchase/lease is being prepared.

23. A consumer hires a broker to serve as a buyer's agent. The broker currently has a property exclusively listed for sale that fully meets the buyer prospect's needs. Which of the following best describes the responsibility of the broker in this situation?

    1. The broker is required to designate one salesperson to represent the buyer prospect and a different salesperson to represent the seller whose property is listed with the broker.
    2. Since the broker already represents the seller, the broker cannot enter into a buyer agency contract with regard to the listed property.
    3. The broker must refer the buyer to a cooperating broker on a referral basis if the buyer wants representation.
    4. Following disclosures required at the initial interview, the broker must secure the written consent of both parties in order to act as a dual agent.

24. A licensed real estate salesperson owns a three-unit apartment building for investment purposes. Under what conditions may the salesperson sell the property?

    1. The salesperson may be a for sale by owner, but the salesperson must disclose his or her license status in advertisements for the property.
    2. The salesperson must list the property for sale with the salesperson's employing broker.
    3. Since the seller is a licensee, only buyers represented by other agents may be shown the property.
    4. The licensee must disclose his or her license status to the buyer at the closing when funds are being disbursed.

25. A consumer contacts a licensee to discuss the possibility of the licensee's handling the sale of a property owned by the consumer. The licensee's responsibility is to

    1. provide the consumer with a written guarantee concerning the amount and type of advertising the broker will provide.
    2. advise the consumer that after listing the property for sale, any cooperating broker who shows the property will be acting as a buyer agent.
    3. provide a Consumer Notice to the prospect before engaging in any substantive discussion about real estate needs with the consumer.
    4. advise the seller that all listing contracts must be in writing on forms approved by the Commission.

26. If a licensed salesperson owns multifamily residential property for investment purposes, the salesperson

    1. must deposit collected rents into an escrow account.
    2. must disclose his or her license status to prospective tenants before the tenant enters into a lease agreement.
    3. may pay a referral fee to another salesperson employed by the same broker if the referred prospect leases a unit in the building.
    4. must hire the employing broker as the property manager and conduct all leasing activity through the broker.

27. When discussing the possibility of listing a large parcel of vacant land with an owner, the broker determines that he would like to secure an option to purchase the property. How should the broker proceed?

    1. Include language in the listing contract granting the option to the broker for purchase of the listed property
    2. Arrange to have the owner enter into an option agreement with a straw party selected by the broker in order to avoid a conflict with the seller
    3. Secure an exclusive-right-to-sell long-term listing but refuse to aggressively market the property until his option has expired
    4. Disclose his interest and license status to the owner and discuss terms of the option agreement prior to and distinct from the listing agreement

28. If a licensed salesperson, without the knowledge or consent of the employing broker, violates requirements regarding delivery of a Consumer Notice at the initial interview, what are the consequences?

    1. The broker will have his or her license suspended or revoked for failing to exercise supervision over the licensed salesperson.
    2. The salesperson may have his or her license suspended or revoked.
    3. Unless the consumer files a written complaint with the Commission, neither the broker nor the salesperson is subject to disciplinary proceedings.
    4. As long as the Consumer Notice is signed by the parties prior to entering into an agreement of sale, there is no violation.

29. A seller is required to give a buyer a property condition disclosure in all of the following transactions *EXCEPT*

1. when the seller is not assisted by a real estate licensee.
2. if the seller was the owner/occupant but has not resided in the property for the past year.
3. for a sale of commercial property.
4. if the buyer has occupied the property as a tenant of the seller.

30. In the case of the sale of an existing single-family home, property condition disclosures must be delivered to the buyer

1. prior to the buyer's making a written offer.
2. at the time the seller agrees to the offer.
3. at the time of the home inspection.
4. at the closing.

31. In Pennsylvania, when a broker is listing a home and asks the seller to complete a property condition disclosure, which of the following statements is *TRUE*?

1. The disclosures are optional, and the seller may avoid liability by refusing to make any disclosures about the condition of the property.
2. The required disclosures cover a narrow range of structural conditions only.
3. An agent should assist the seller by providing advice regarding which property conditions to disclose and which to ignore.
4. The seller should be advised that disclosure of known property conditions is required by Pennsylvania statute.

32. Six months after the buyer bought a house, the roof leaked during a rainstorm. When the house was listed, the seller told the broker that the roof leaked, but they agreed not to disclose the fact to prospective buyers. The broker claims that the buyer did not ask about the roof. Under these facts, the buyer

1. may sue the broker and the seller.
2. may not sue the broker because the broker was following the instructions of his principal, the seller.
3. may sue the seller under license law.
4. has no recourse because the leaking roof could have been discovered by conducting a home inspection.

33. All of the following are exempt from the Property Condition Disclosure Act *EXCEPT* a

1. foreclosure sale.
2. new construction sale covered by a builder's warranty.
3. conveyance of a primary residence from one former spouse to another under a divorce settlement agreement.
4. sale by a real estate licensee of a two-unit residential property when it is sold for sale by owner.

34. A real estate broker representing the seller knows that the property has a cracked foundation and that its former owner committed suicide in the kitchen. By law, which fact(s) must the broker disclose to a prospective buyer?

1. Both facts
2. The suicide, but not the cracked foundation
3. The cracked foundation, but not the suicide
4. Neither fact

35. Five years ago, unit 5B in a condominium community was the site of a brutal and highly publicized murder. The unit was sold to an elderly woman who contracted the AIDS virus in a blood transfusion and died in the unit last year. As the agent for the woman's estate, what are your disclosure responsibilities to prospective purchasers of unit 5B in this situation?

    1. You must disclose both the murder and the AIDS-related death.
    2. You are specifically prohibited by law from disclosing either event.
    3. You are not required to disclose either event.
    4. You are not required to disclose the murder, but you must disclose the AIDS-related death.

36. How are members of the Pennsylvania Real Estate Commission selected?

    1. Appointed by the governor
    2. Public election
    3. By a committee of the state Association of REALTORS®
    4. Elected by real estate licensees

37. In order to become a member of the Pennsylvania Real Estate Commission, a candidate must

    1. be endorsed by the state and local associations of REALTORS®.
    2. be appointed by the governor.
    3. be a licensed broker or salesperson actively engaged in the real estate business.
    4. post a surety bond in the amount of $10,000.

38. How many members of the Pennsylvania Real Estate Commission are required to be licensed real estate brokers at the time of their appointment?

    1. 11
    2. 9
    3. 6
    4. 5

39. All of the following statements regarding the Pennsylvania Real Estate Commission are true *EXCEPT*

    1. members of the Commission are selected by the state Association of REALTORS®.
    2. the Commission makes and enforces the rules by which real estate licensees must abide.
    3. the examinations that must be taken by applicants for real estate licensing are administered by an independent testing company rather than by the Commission.
    4. the Commission must submit annual reports to legislative committees in the state senate and house of representatives.

40. In Pennsylvania, the real estate license law is administered by the

    1. Department of State.
    2. Real Estate Commission.
    3. state Association of REALTORS®.
    4. Department of Housing and Urban Development.

41. The purpose of the license law is to

    1. prevent convicted criminals from engaging in the real estate business.
    2. generate license and renewal fees for the state treasury.
    3. authorize the Pennsylvania Real Estate Commission to promulgate rules and regulations.
    4. ensure that the public interest is protected.

42. The Pennsylvania Real Estate Commission has the authority to

    1. make and enforce the rules by which all real estate licensees must abide.
    2. compose the examination questions on the state exam.
    3. administer the exams given at the testing sites.
    4. enact the laws that govern real estate licensees.

43. The Pennsylvania Real Estate Commission may undertake an investigation of a licensee based on all the following grounds *EXCEPT*

    1. its own initiative.
    2. a random selection of licensees currently active.
    3. a motion from the members of the Commission.
    4. a written complaint submitted by a consumer.

44. During the course of a routine or special inspection, the Commission or its authorized representative will be permitted to do all of the following *EXCEPT*

    1. interview consumers who are presently conducting business during the inspection.
    2. examine records of the office pertaining to real estate transactions.
    3. inspect all areas of the office.
    4. obtain written authorization to access records of the broker's escrow account.

45. The Pennsylvania Real Estate Commission has statutory authority to perform all of the following duties *EXCEPT*

    1. prescribe the subjects to be tested on license examinations.
    2. approve schools offering or conducting courses of study in real estate.
    3. waive all or part of the continuing education requirement for a salesperson or broker due to illness, emergency, or hardship.
    4. issue licenses and registration certificates to persons who comply with provisions established by the license law.

46. Who of the following is subject to disciplinary action by the Pennsylvania Real Estate Commission?

    1. Employees of a real estate appraisal firm
    2. Elected officers of a banking institution handling real estate transactions for the bank
    3. An attorney-in-fact rendering services under an executed and recorded power of attorney
    4. Campground membership salesperson

47. A salesperson has engaged in activities that constitute several violations of the Pennsylvania Human Relations Act, including blockbusting and discrimination on the basis of disability. The salesperson has also cashed a $25,000 earnest money check from a prospective buyer and used the proceeds to buy a new car. The salesperson's employing broker was unaware of all of these activities. What is the impact on the employing broker's license when the salesperson's violations are brought to the attention of the Pennsylvania Real Estate Commission?

    1. The employing broker might not have his or her license revoked as a result of the salesperson's violations.
    2. The salesperson's employing broker will be required to pay any fine imposed against the salesperson out of his or her personal funds.
    3. The salesperson's actions are legally the responsibility of the employing broker, who will be subject to the same disciplinary action as the salesperson regardless of whether he or she knew the violations had occurred.
    4. The salesperson's employing broker will be held liable for the Human Relations Act violations only.

48. Which of the following actions on the part of the broker are legal and *NOT* a violation of the license law?

    1. Openly soliciting salespeople or associate brokers employed by competitors to change employing brokers
    2. Placing a For Sale sign or advertising property for sale without the written consent of the owner
    3. Failing to specify a definite termination date that is not subject to prior notice in a listing contract
    4. Failing to exercise adequate supervision over the activities of licensed salespeople who are independent contractors

49. The Pennsylvania Real Estate Commission may take disciplinary action against a licensee when the licensee violates all of the following *EXCEPT*

    1. the Pennsylvania Human Relations Act.
    2. rules and regulations adopted by the Pennsylvania Real Estate Commission.
    3. the Real Estate Licensing and Registration Act.
    4. the Sherman Antitrust Act.

50. A listing broker offers a $500 bonus to any salesperson who sells a particular listing within the next 30 days. Which of the following is *TRUE*?

    1. The seller must give his consent in writing to the broker allowing him to offer the bonus.
    2. The broker may only pay the bonus to a salesperson who is employed by the listing broker.
    3. The broker may directly pay the bonus to a salesperson employed by another broker with the consent of the other broker.
    4. A bonus for selling property must be paid to the salesperson directly by the seller rather than the broker.

51. Which of the following activities would most likely result in disciplinary action against a broker?

    1. Allowing a newly licensed salesperson to hold open houses for the public before completing the company's training program
    2. Paying a bonus directly to a licensed salesperson employed by another licensed broker
    3. Requiring associate brokers in the broker's employ to agree to noncompete clauses in their employment contracts
    4. Having a salesperson employed by the broker found guilty of making a misrepresentation, even if the broker had no knowledge of the misrepresentation

52. A broker is convicted of felony possession and distribution of a controlled substance. Both the crime and the conviction took place out of state. After 30 days, the broker calls the Pennsylvania Real Estate Commission and leaves a message informing the Commission of the conviction. Based on these facts, which of the following is *TRUE*?

    1. The broker has properly informed the Pennsylvania Real Estate Commission after the conviction, and the broker's license will not be affected.
    2. Both the conviction and the broker's failure to properly notify the Commission within 30 days of the conviction are grounds for suspension or revocation of the broker's license.
    3. Because the conviction did not occur in Pennsylvania, it is not grounds for suspending or revoking the broker's license.
    4. The conviction is evidence of both improper dealing and fraud.

53. As a result of a hearing alleging a violation of the license law, what action may the Real Estate Commission take?

    1. Suspend or revoke any license issued by it
    2. Levy a fine not to exceed $500
    3. Suspend the license and impose a fine
    4. Impose a maximum sentence of up to three months in prison

54. If a licensee is found guilty of making substantial misrepresentation when dealing with the public, the Commission may

    1. levy a fine of up to $5,000.
    2. impose a jail sentence of up to three months.
    3. revoke the licensee's license and/or impose a fine.
    4. suspend the licensee's license or levy a fine but not do both for the same offense.

55. An individual is found guilty of engaging in business as a broker or salesperson without being properly licensed. The penalty for the first offense includes

    1. a fine of up to $5,000 and imprisonment for a maximum of two years.
    2. a fine of up to $500, imprisonment for a maximum of three months, or both.
    3. a fine of up to $1,000.
    4. a fine of up to $1,000 or three months in prison.

56. What is the maximum penalty that may be imposed on an individual found guilty for the second time of engaging in the real estate business without a license?

    1. A fine of $5,000 and imprisonment for a period of two years
    2. Imprisonment for three months
    3. A fine of $1,000
    4. A fine of $2,000 and imprisonment for one year

57. In Pennsylvania, all of the following would be grounds for revoking a broker's license *EXCEPT*

    1. being convicted of a felony.
    2. advertising in a newspaper that he or she is a member of the Pennsylvania Association of Real Estate Professionals when in fact he or she is not.
    3. depositing a buyer's earnest money into the salesperson's personal checking account.
    4. agreeing with a seller to accept a listing for more than the company's normal commission rate.

58. In Pennsylvania, which of the following is legal and will not result in a broker's facing suspension or revocation of the broker's license?

    1. Being legally declared mentally incompetent
    2. Depositing earnest money received into the firm's escrow account
    3. Helping another person cheat on the licensing examination
    4. Displaying a For Sale sign on a property without the owner's written consent

59. When is the Pennsylvania Real Estate Commission required to suspend a licensee's license?

    1. If the licensee fails to perform as promised in a guaranteed sales plan
    2. If the licensee is found liable in a civil trial for illegal discrimination
    3. If the licensee commingles others' money or property with his or her own
    4. If any amount of money had been paid from the Real Estate Recovery Fund to settle a claim against the licensee

60. Which of the following actions is legal and *NOT* a violation of license law?

    1. Encouraging a seller to reject an offer because the prospective buyer is of a specific religion
    2. Placing a For Sale sign in front of a house after receiving written permission to do so from the owner
    3. Advertising that individuals who attend a promotional presentation will receive a prize without mentioning that they will also have to take a day trip to a new subdivision site
    4. Allowing salespeople employed by a broker to maintain their own escrow accounts

61. When a sole proprietor broker has her license suspended for two years, what effect does this have on the associate brokers and salespeople affiliated with the broker?

    1. Affiliates' licenses will be revoked, subject to reinstatement after one year
    2. Affiliates' licenses will also be suspended for a two-year period
    3. Suspension has no effect on the affiliates
    4. Affiliates' licenses are terminated

62. In what circumstance may a violation of the license law on the part of a salesperson be grounds for the suspension or revocation of the employing broker's license?

    1. The broker's license is only subject to suspension or revocation if the broker participated with the salesperson in violating the license law.
    2. The broker's license is subject to suspension or revocation if it can be shown that the broker had actual knowledge of the violation committed by the salesperson.
    3. Because the salesperson is employed by the broker, the broker's license is always subject to suspension or revocation as a result of any violation on the part of the salesperson.
    4. Only the licensee actually found to have violated the license law may have a license suspended or revoked, so the broker's license may not be suspended or revoked because of the salesperson's misconduct.

63. If a licensee has had his license revoked, how many years must he wait before reapplying for licensure?

    1. 3
    2. 5
    3. 7
    4. 10

64. When is a violation of the license law on the part of a salesperson grounds for revocation or suspension of the license of the employing broker?

    1. If it can be shown that the conduct that resulted in the disciplinary action was a common course of dealing for that salesperson
    2. Only if the salesperson was an employee rather than an independent contractor
    3. Only if the employing broker and the licensed salesperson worked from the same office of the broker
    4. Only if the offense involved monetary damage to a consumer

65. A broker who wishes to place a For Sale sign on a listed property must first

    1. obtain the written consent of the owner of the property.
    2. sell the property.
    3. secure an exclusive-listing contract from the seller.
    4. get permission from the neighbors and the local governing body.

66. When advertising real property for sale, real estate salespeople

    1. need only include the salesperson's personal phone number.
    2. may simply give a phone number to call for more information.
    3. must include the name of the employing broker in the advertisement.
    4. must identify the location of the property.

67. A real estate salesperson decides to sell her own property for sale by owner. When advertising the property, the salesperson

    1. must disclose the name, address, and phone number of her employing broker.
    2. must disclose in the advertisement the fact that she is a real estate licensee.
    3. if acting as a for sale by owner, does not need to disclose her license status in the advertisement.
    4. is prohibited from advertising as a for sale by owner.

68. When a broker advertises his production or position in the market, what must be included in the advertisement?

    1. Number of licensed branch offices that the broker maintains in the market
    2. Municipality that the market comprises
    3. Dollar volume of sales transactions written in the market
    4. Number of cooperating brokers that engage in business in the market

69. When advertising an individual property for sale, the broker must also include

    1. the price of the property being advertised.
    2. a statement or logo affirming the broker's commitment to nondiscriminatory business practices.
    3. the business name of the broker as designated on the license.
    4. the name and business phone number of the listing salesperson or associate broker.

70. When advertising property for sale, what must the broker include in the advertisement?

    1. Listing price of the property
    2. Name of the salesperson who secured the listing
    3. Broker's business name designated on the license
    4. Disclosure statement identifying who the broker is representing

71. A broker has developed a Web site advertising the broker's office. What, if anything, does the broker need to include?

    1. Name as it appears on the license
    2. License number of brokerage and list of all current active licensees
    3. Names of active licensees with addresses and phone numbers
    4. There is no need for any disclosure.

72. A licensed salesperson secures a listing and wants to advertise it on the salesperson's own Web site. Which of the following must the salesperson comply with when advertising on the Internet?

    1. A complete description of the property, including address and price, must be included in the advertising.
    2. The advertisement must contain the business's name and the phone number of the employing broker.
    3. The salesperson must have the specific written permission of the owner to advertise the property on the Internet rather than in traditional advertising sources.
    4. The salesperson may not advertise on a Web site unless the broker maintains a company Web site for purposes of advertising all of the company's listings.

73. Three weeks before Ned begins his real estate prelicense class, he offers to help his neighbor sell her house. The neighbor agrees to pay him a 5 percent commission. The seller accepts an offer while Ned is taking the class and closes the day he passes the examination. The neighbor refuses to pay Ned the agreed commission. Can Ned sue to recover payment?

    1. Yes, because Ned was formally enrolled in a course of study intended to result in a real estate license at the time an offer was procured and accepted, the commission agreement is binding.
    2. No, a real estate salesperson must have a permanent office in which his or her license is displayed in order to collect a commission from a seller.
    3. Yes, while the statute of frauds forbids recovery on an oral agreement for the conveyance of real property, the law permits enforcement of an oral commission contract under these facts.
    4. No, license law prohibits lawsuits to collect commissions unless the injured party was properly licensed at the time the agreement was reached.

74. An unlicensed individual who engages in activities for which a real estate license is required is subject to which penalty upon conviction for a first offense?

    1. Fine not to exceed $500
    2. Fine not to exceed $1,000 and one-year imprisonment
    3. Civil penalty of $5,000 in addition to other penalties provided by law
    4. A fine not to exceed $5,000 and a mandatory prison term not to exceed five years

75. An individual wants to sell her own house. In this situation, the individual

    1. does not need a real estate license to sell her house herself.
    2. must first obtain a real estate license issued by the Pennsylvania Real Estate Commission.
    3. may obtain a temporary real estate license in order to legally sell her house.
    4. may sell her house without obtaining a real estate license only if she is a licensed attorney.

76. An unlicensed salesperson negotiated the sale of real estate in return for the promise of compensation. After the transaction closes, the salesperson encounters difficulty collecting the agreed-upon fee. In this situation, the salesperson

    1. may record a lien against the property for the amount owed.
    2. may file a civil lawsuit against the seller in the court of common pleas in the county where the property is located.
    3. may file a claim for compensation from the Real Estate Recovery Fund.
    4. may do nothing to recover the agreed-upon compensation.

77. An officer of a corporation is designated by the corporation to handle the sale of a parcel of real estate owned by the corporation. Which of the following statements is *TRUE* regarding the corporate officer handling the sale of real estate owned by the corporation?

    1. Unless the corporate officer is a licensed broker, he or she may not handle the sale of real estate owned by the corporation.
    2. The corporate officer must be the president and CEO of the corporation to engage in business on behalf of the corporation.
    3. The corporation, as the owner of real estate, may designate up to five of its officers to conduct business on behalf of the corporation without any license required.
    4. The corporate officer may handle the sale only if there is no compensation involved.

78. A broker personally owns a ten-unit residential, multifamily property. The broker hires an unlicensed individual for the purpose of managing and maintaining the property. The unlicensed individual may legally perform which of the following activities?

    1. Show apartments to prospective tenants and provide information on rental amounts and leasing determination
    2. Enter into leases on behalf of the owner
    3. Negotiate terms or conditions of occupancy with current or prospective tenants
    4. Supervise and direct a branch office of the broker located at the property

79. A foreign corporation that owns a building in Pennsylvania decides to sell without listing it for sale. Who may legally handle the transaction on behalf of the corporation?

    1. Only a licensed Pennsylvania broker may handle the sale of property owned by a foreign corporation.
    2. A licensed broker in the state where the corporation is headquartered may handle the sale without being licensed in Pennsylvania.
    3. A licensed Pennsylvania salesperson may be directly employed by the corporation to handle the transaction.
    4. An attorney-at-law who renders services to the corporation within the scope of an attorney-client relationship may handle the transaction for the corporation.

80. An unlicensed individual acting as a real estate consultant negotiated a sale of property and was unable to collect the agreed-upon fee from the seller. The unlicensed individual

    1. may file a lawsuit for breach of contract in the court of common pleas in the county where the land is located.
    2. may seek compensation from the Real Estate Recovery Fund for the unpaid fee.
    3. has no recourse under the law because a person who holds himself out as a real estate consultant is required to have a broker's license.
    4. may record a judgment against the owner if the contract contained a confession of judgment clause.

81. A salesperson remains inactive without renewing his license for over five years. Before the license will be reissued, the applicant must

    1. complete 60 hours of coursework and pass the salesperson's license exam.
    2. complete 14 hours of mandatory continuing education with no exam requirement.
    3. submit to and pass the salesperson's license examination.
    4. successfully complete the employing broker's training program.

82. A broker operating as a sole proprietor wants to locate the main office of his business at his personal residence. In this case, all of the following requirements would apply *EXCEPT*

    1. the office must be devoted to the transaction of real estate business and be arranged to permit business to be conducted in privacy.
    2. the entrance to the office must be separate from the entrance to the residence.
    3. the business name of the broker as designated on the license must be displayed prominently and in permanent fashion outside the office.
    4. the broker may not employ salespeople or associate brokers to work at an office in a personal residence.

83. In Pennsylvania, which of the following would need to be a licensed real estate broker or salesperson?

    1. A property management company that employs fewer than three leasing agents
    2. A licensed attorney acting under a power of attorney to convey real estate
    3. A resident apartment manager employed by an owner when showing apartments to prospective tenants
    4. A partnership selling a building owned by the partners

84. Under Pennsylvania licensing law, a partnership, association, or corporation will be granted a broker's license only if

    1. one officer or partner is designated as the broker of record.
    2. every member and officer actively participating in the brokerage business has a broker's license.
    3. all license papers are filed with the Secretary of State.
    4. the brokerage business has paid a one-time fee to the recovery fund.

85. An applicant for a real estate salesperson's license in Pennsylvania must

    1. have completed at least two years of college.
    2. be at least 21 years old.
    3. not have been convicted of a felony within five years before applying.
    4. show proof of passing the license examination within three years of the date of application for licensure.

86. Some people and situations are exempt from the provisions of the Pennsylvania Real Estate License Act. Which of the following persons is not exempt and must hold a real estate license?

    1. Property owner who sells or leases his or her own property
    2. Individual who receives compensation from sellers or landlords for procuring prospective buyers or renters of real estate
    3. Individual who is employed directly by an owner as a resident property manager for an apartment complex
    4. Licensed auctioneer handling the sale of real estate at a bona fide auction

87. Which of the following is a requirement to obtain a real estate salesperson's license in Pennsylvania?

    1. Successful completion of 14 credit hours of real estate law, finance, and appraisal
    2. An associate degree in real estate from an accredited college, university, or proprietary school
    3. U.S. citizenship
    4. Successful completion of 60 classroom hours of instruction in courses prescribed by the Commission

88. An individual directly employed by the owner of residential multifamily buildings is exempt from licensing requirements when

    1. showing apartments to prospective tenants and explaining building rules and regulations.
    2. preparing and entering into leases on behalf of the building's owner.
    3. negotiating terms or conditions of occupancy with current tenants.
    4. holding money belonging to tenants other than on behalf of the building's owner.

89. An applicant for a broker's license must

    1. post a performance bond in the amount of $10,000.
    2. be a resident of the Commonwealth of Pennsylvania.
    3. have been actively engaged in selling real estate for at least three years.
    4. be a high school graduate or provide proof of equivalent education.

90. A candidate for a broker's license in Pennsylvania must

    1. be a college graduate.
    2. be a citizen of the United States.
    3. have experience in real estate sales.
    4. have passed the broker's license exam within three years prior to license application.

91. Which of the following candidates for licensure is required to take the standard real estate salesperson's license examination and score a passing grade but is *NOT* required to complete any mandatory education requirement prior to taking the exam?

    1. Builder-owner salesperson applicant
    2. Cemetery salesperson applicant
    3. Rental listing referral license applicant
    4. Campground membership salesperson license applicant

92. Which of the following applicants for licensure is *NOT* required to pass a written exam for licensure?

    1. Builder-owner salesperson
    2. Rental listing referral agent
    3. Cemetery salesperson
    4. Cemetery broker

93. All of the following persons must complete education or training requirements prior to licensure *EXCEPT*

    1. campground membership salespeople.
    2. time-share salespeople.
    3. cemetery salespeople.
    4. rental listing referral agents.

94. In order to qualify for examination as a broker, the candidate must

    1. be a high school graduate or have passed a high school general equivalency examination.
    2. have been actively employed as a licensed salesperson for at least three years.
    3. be a resident of Pennsylvania.
    4. submit recommendations from at least two brokers licensed in Pennsylvania.

95. Of the following licensed individuals, who must complete 14 hours of mandatory continuing education as a condition of license renewal?

    1. Licensed time-share or campground membership salesperson
    2. Licensed builder-owner salesperson
    3. Licensed broker of record of a corporation or partnership listing and selling real estate
    4. Licensed cemetery broker

96. When do real estate salespersons' licenses expire in Pennsylvania?

    1. Biennially, in the month issued
    2. May 31 of every even-numbered year
    3. December 31 of the third year of licensure
    4. Two years from the date the license was issued

97. To renew a license in Pennsylvania, a salesperson or broker must

    1. prove that he or she is a Pennsylvania resident.
    2. be actively participating in the real estate business.
    3. have completed six hours of continuing education in the last two years, composed of three hours in real estate law and three hours in fair housing.
    4. complete 14 hours of continuing education and pay the appropriate renewal fee.

98. The term *broker* includes in its definition all of the following activities *EXCEPT*

    1. managing real estate.
    2. appraising real estate.
    3. representing oneself as a real estate consultant or counselor.
    4. performing a comparative market analysis.

99. Which of the following persons must have a real estate broker's license in order to transact real estate business?

    1. The owner of a six-unit building who manages it personally, collects rents, and shows the apartments to prospective tenants
    2. One who negotiates the sale of entire businesses, including their stock, equipment, and buildings, for a promised fee
    3. The manager of a large apartment building who is directly employed by the owner and who shows apartments to prospective tenants as part of his or her regular duties
    4. One who has power of attorney to negotiate the sale of his or her parent's residence

100. The on-site property manager employed directly by the owner of Acme Apartments is responsible for collecting rents for the apartments. In this position, the on-site manager

    1. must have a salesperson's license.
    2. must have a broker's license.
    3. is exempt from the licensing requirements.
    4. is not required to be licensed if he or she is an independent contractor.

101. At what point may a candidate for a salesperson's license begin to engage in activities for which a license is required?

    1. Immediately upon passing the license examination
    2. Upon completion of the prelicense education requirement if the activity is directly supervised by a broker
    3. On the day the employing broker sends the license application and appropriate fee to the Commission
    4. Only after a license has been issued by the state to the salesperson

102. A licensed real estate salesperson may engage in all of the following activities on behalf of her employing broker *EXCEPT*

    1. perform an appraisal for a federally related mortgage loan.
    2. negotiate the purchase, sale, or exchange of commercial real estate.
    3. assist the broker in the management of residential multifamily real estate.
    4. negotiate a loan on real estate.

103. Immediately upon passing the salesperson licensing examination, which of the following activities may an individual legally engage in?

    1. Selling business opportunities to the public
    2. Holding open houses for the public under the direct supervision of a broker
    3. Preparing and presenting a comparative market analysis to a prospective seller
    4. Negotiating a loan on real estate on behalf of a broker

104. Rental listing referral agents are licensed to engage in which of the following activities?

    1. Showing residential rental units in multifamily housing to prospective tenants
    2. Collecting rental information for the purpose of referring prospective tenants to rental units or locations of rental units
    3. Engaging in commercial property management activities on behalf of more than one employing broker at the same time
    4. Collecting rental application fees and security deposits on behalf of an owner of rental property

105. Which of the following activities may a builder-owner salesperson employed by a builder-owner of single and multifamily dwellings legally engage in?

    1. Leasing a newly constructed home owned by his employer to a prospective tenant
    2. Negotiating a mortgage loan on behalf of a buyer purchasing one of his employer's homes
    3. Listing for sale a property owned by a purchaser who wants to purchase one of the builder's model homes
    4. Collecting referral fees from real estate brokers in return for listing leads

106. Real estate licensing is required in order to engage in the

    1. sale of time-share interests.
    2. negotiation of leases by employees of a public utility.
    3. sale of property by an individual acting as a trustee in a bankruptcy proceeding.
    4. sale of real estate by a licensed auctioneer at a bona fide auction.

107. In reference to license laws and rules and regulations of the Commission, what does the term *broker of record* refer to?

    1. An employing broker who employs other associate brokers to work on his or her behalf
    2. An individual broker responsible for the real estate transactions of a partnership, association, or corporation that holds a broker's license
    3. A sole proprietor who maintains multiple branch offices and hires associate brokers to manage those offices
    4. An associate broker authorized to directly control and supervise activities at a licensed branch office

108. Regarding licensing and employment of personal real estate assistants in Pennsylvania, the personal assistant

    1. must always be licensed.
    2. may deposit and withdraw funds from the broker's escrow account without being licensed.
    3. may host open houses for the public only if he or she is licensed.
    4. must be employed by the broker rather than directly by a salesperson.

109. A salesperson's licensed assistant worked late nights and weekends to help ensure the successful completion of a difficult transaction. The assistant's extra work included making several phone calls to the prospective buyers and encouraging them to accept the seller's counteroffer. Largely because of the assistant's efforts, the sale went through with no problem. The salesperson wants to pay the assistant a percentage of the commission "because the assistant has really earned it." Under Pennsylvania law, the salesperson may

    1. directly compensate the assistant in the form of a commission under the circumstances described here.
    2. not pay the assistant a cash commission but is permitted to make a gift of tangible personal property.
    3. not directly pay a commission to the assistant under the facts presented here because it would be a violation of the license law.
    4. directly pay a commission to the assistant only if the assistant is an independent contractor.

110. An individual who holds a salesperson's license issued by another jurisdiction wants to obtain a Pennsylvania salesperson's license. Which of the following requirements must be met?

    1. The salesperson's license issued by another jurisdiction must have been active within five years prior to the submission of a properly completed application.
    2. The individual must score a passing grade on both parts of the Pennsylvania salesperson's license examination.
    3. The individual must prove that the license issued by another jurisdiction has been put on inactive status by that jurisdiction.
    4. The individual must establish legal residency in Pennsylvania.

111. A real estate salesperson has been working with buyer clients and helps them negotiate for their dream home. The buyer then asks the salesperson if she can help them secure a mortgage loan. The salesperson knows a lender that pays a fee for referring purchasers to them. Can the salesperson refer the buyers to this lender in order to collect the referral fee?

   1. No, because the salesperson would be violating the license law by accepting compensation from someone other than her employing broker
   2. Yes, if the salesperson and the buyers have previously entered into a written buyer agency agreement
   3. No, unless the salesperson first discloses the referral fee to the buyers
   4. Yes, if the lender offers the best interest rates and terms available in the market

112. Under the terms of a sales contract, the seller is required to pay for and provide a termite certificate. The seller requests that the salesperson order one. The salesperson does so, knowing he will receive a referral fee directly from the pest control company. The referral fee is not discussed with the seller. Is this a violation of the license law?

   1. No, if the fee is less than $25
   2. No, if the fee is split with the broker
   3. Yes, because the licensee did not disclose the compensation to the consumer
   4. Yes, because fees may be paid to the salesperson only by the seller

113. An airline pilot told a broker about some friends who were looking for a new home. The broker contacted the friends and eventually sold them a house. When may the broker pay the airline pilot a referral fee?

   1. As soon as a valid sales contract is signed by the parties
   2. Only after the sale closes
   3. As soon as the broker begins working with the buyer prospect
   4. Never, because a broker may not pay a referral fee to an unlicensed individual

114. A buyer has just entered into a contract to buy a time-share interest in a unit from the developer. This new buyer has a right to cancel the contract

   1. within three days from the date the buyer's attorney reviews the documents.
   2. any time during the period agreed upon by the buyer and developer in the contract.
   3. within five days from the date the new buyer executed the contract.
   4. at no time because the buyer has entered into a binding contract.

115. A couple visited a time-share property and received a gift of a portable color television for signing a purchase agreement for a time-share interest that day. Four days later, the couple decided not to go through with the transaction. Under what circumstances may they void the contract?

   1. Although the couple may cancel the purchase agreement, they must return the portable color television.
   2. The couple is bound to the terms of the purchase agreement and does not have the right to cancel the purchase.
   3. The couple may cancel the purchase agreement until midnight of the fifth day following the purchase, and they may keep the portable color television.
   4. Because it is illegal to offer promotional prizes and gifts as an inducement, the purchase agreement is void.

116. In Pennsylvania, brokers and salespeople may

   1. bind the principal they represent to contracts.
   2. fill in blanks on preprinted contract forms customarily used in their community.
   3. write additional language for the purpose of modifying a sales contract between a buyer and seller after advising them of the legal consequences of the new language.
   4. give advice concerning the legal significance of specific preprinted contract clauses to a buyer or seller.

117. Which of the following could be construed as the unauthorized practice of law?

    1. Informing the buyer of the broker's personal opinion of the condition of the seller's title to the property
    2. Making sure that the written agreement of sale includes a statement as to whether the broker is the agent of the seller or the agent of the buyer
    3. Providing each party with a written estimate of reasonably foreseeable expenses associated with the sale before the agreement of sale is executed
    4. Keeping copies of all documents involved in the transaction on file for three years after consummation of the transaction

118. Unless the parties to the agreement of sale agree otherwise, earnest money deposits received by a broker on behalf of her principal must be deposited in an escrow account

    1. three days after receiving the offer.
    2. three days after obtaining all signatures on the contract.
    3. five working days after receiving the offer.
    4. by the end of the next business day following its receipt in the office where the escrow records are maintained.

119. A broker received an earnest money deposit from a buyer. Under Pennsylvania law, the broker should

    1. open a special, separate escrow account that will contain funds for this transaction only, separate from funds received in any other transaction.
    2. deposit the money in an existing escrow account in which all earnest money received from buyers may be held at the same time.
    3. immediately (or by the next business day) deposit the earnest money in the broker's personal interest-bearing checking or savings account.
    4. hold the earnest money deposit in a secure place in the broker's real estate brokerage office until the transaction closes.

120. The broker received a buyer's earnest money check for $5,000 and immediately cashed it. At closing, the broker handed the seller a personal check for $5,300, representing the original earnest money plus 6 percent interest. The broker

    1. should have deposited the check in a special escrow account at a bank or recognized depository.
    2. properly cashed the check but should have kept the interest.
    3. should have deposited the money in his personal bank account and kept the interest as a service fee.
    4. should have written a check for $5,000 to the seller and a separate check for $300 to the buyer.

121. A licensed salesperson negotiates an offer to purchase on a property listed for sale with a different company. The buyer gives the salesperson an earnest money deposit check. The salesperson

    1. must deposit the check in an escrow account maintained in the salesperson's own name at a bank or recognized depository.
    2. is required to deliver the earnest money deposit to the listing broker for deposit.
    3. retains the check in his or her file until the offer is accepted by the seller.
    4. is required to pay the deposit to the salesperson's employing broker promptly upon receipt.

122. Every licensed broker is required to

    1. maintain escrow account records for five years.
    2. keep transaction records for three years.
    3. become a member of the local Association of REALTORS®.
    4. employ at least one salesperson.

123. How long must a real estate broker keep records relating to real estate transactions?

    1. One year from the date the property was listed with the broker
    2. Three years following consummation of the transaction
    3. Indefinitely
    4. Until the transaction closes and title passes from the seller to the buyer

124. A broker is employed as a property manager. The building owner and the broker agree that the building's air-conditioning system needs to be replaced, and the broker is authorized to contract for the work to be done. Without the owner's knowledge, the broker and the contractor chosen to do the work agree that as a condition of receiving the contract, the contractor will install central air-conditioning in the personal residence of the broker at no charge to the broker. Could this action result in disciplinary action against the broker by the Commission?

    1. No, because the broker has been authorized by the owner to contract to have the work done
    2. Yes, because accepting any undisclosed compensation or profit for expenditures on behalf of an owner is a violation of the license law
    3. Yes, because only the owner is authorized to contract for work to be done on the building he or she owns
    4. No, because terms of the contract between the broker and contractor are not an issue of concern to the Pennsylvania Real Estate Commission

125. Under what circumstances may a broker deposit personal or business funds into his or her escrow account?

    1. Never; commingling personal or business funds with escrow funds is prohibited.
    2. The broker may deposit personal or business funds in an escrow account to cover service charges assessed to the account or to maintain a minimum balance as required by the bank.
    3. The broker may deposit such funds if the broker maintains one account that serves as both the personal or business account and an escrow account simultaneously.
    4. The broker may make such a deposit only if it appears he or she will not be able to deposit the funds in the personal or business account by close of business of the next business day.

126. A licensed broker is employed by the owner of a residential multifamily housing complex to serve as the property manager. One of the broker's duties is to collect rent due from the tenants. When the rents are collected, the broker should

    1. deposit rents received into a rental management account that is separate from the broker's escrow account and general business account.
    2. immediately deliver the rents to the owner of the complex for deposit in the owner's business account.
    3. deposit the rents into his or her escrow account because they are the property of the owner.
    4. deposit them into his or her personal or business account to cover the cost of repairs and maintenance at the complex.

127. Who has authority to withdraw funds from the broker's escrow account for payments that are properly chargeable to the account?

    1. A licensed employee who has been given written authority by the employing broker
    2. An unlicensed accountant or bookkeeper who is an employee of the broker
    3. The principal broker is the only one with authority to withdraw funds from his or her escrow account
    4. A settlement officer employed by a title company when disbursing funds at a closing

128. When a selling broker negotiates a sale of property listed by a cooperating broker, who is responsible for assuming the duties regarding escrow of the buyer's deposit check?

    1. The listing broker representing the seller is required to hold the deposit in his or her escrow account.
    2. The selling broker is required to hold the buyer's deposit in escrow if acting as the buyer's agent.
    3. If the buyer gives the sales deposit to the listing broker rather than to the selling broker, the listing broker assumes the escrow duty.
    4. The rules of the local multiple listing service dictate which broker will hold the escrow deposit.

129. Which of the following statements is *TRUE* regarding the broker's escrow account?

    1. The escrow account may designate the broker's company attorney as trustee of the account.
    2. The escrow account must be an interest-bearing account.
    3. Upon written request of the Commission, the broker must provide a letter authorizing release of records pertaining to the account.
    4. Brokers acting as property managers may deposit rents collected into the escrow account until they can be paid to the building owner.

130. Regarding a broker's escrow account,

    1. as long as all parties to the transaction agree in writing, the broker's escrow duty may be waived.
    2. if a dispute arises between the parties over entitlement to the money that is held in escrow, the broker retains the money in escrow until the dispute is resolved.
    3. funds received must be deposited in the broker's escrow account by the end of the next business day following their receipt by the salesperson involved in the transaction.
    4. the account must be an interest-bearing account if the funds will be held for more than six months.

131. A licensed salesperson receives an earnest money deposit check from a buyer at the time the buyer makes an offer to purchase property listed by another broker. The seller is unavailable, so the offer will not be presented for four days. What procedure should be followed regarding the earnest money deposit check?

    1. Because the duty to escrow funds does not begin until the agreement of sale is signed by all parties, the salesperson may keep the check in the file with the offer to purchase until the offer is presented.
    2. The salesperson is responsible for immediately depositing the check into the company escrow account.
    3. The selling broker must deliver the earnest money check to the listing broker, who will be responsible for depositing it.
    4. If written permission of both buyer and seller has been obtained, the broker may refrain from depositing the check pending the seller's acceptance of the offer.

132. Regarding interest paid on an escrow account maintained by the broker, interest earned on an escrow account

    1. is disbursed in the same manner as the principal amount unless the parties to the transaction agree otherwise.
    2. does not begin to accrue on the deposit until it has been held in the broker's escrow account for at least six months.
    3. belongs to the broker as compensation for managing and maintaining the account on behalf of buyers and sellers.
    4. may not be earned on escrow accounts because of the difficulty in allocating the interest to the appropriate parties.

133. A purchaser tenders an earnest money deposit check with an offer to purchase and instructs the salesperson not to deposit the check until the seller accepts the offer. What should the salesperson do?

    1. If the salesperson is a buyer's agent, the salesperson must follow the instruction of the buyer and refrain from depositing the check.
    2. The deposit check must be deposited by the end of the next business day following its receipt.
    3. If both the buyer and the seller have given written permission, the deposit check may be held pending the seller's acceptance of the offer.
    4. The salesperson may refrain from depositing the check only if the broker's office policy permits such conduct.

134. A licensed broker receives an earnest money deposit from a buyer and promptly deposits it in an interest-bearing account opened at a local bank in the name of the seller. The buyer is provided with the account number, verification of the deposit, the seller's name, and the name of the bank. Which of the following statements is *TRUE?*

    1. The broker acted properly by providing all information about the deposit to both parties to the transaction.
    2. The broker should have opened the account in the names of both the buyer and the seller.
    3. The broker should have deposited the funds in an escrow account maintained in his or her name and identifying the broker as trustee.
    4. The deposit must be available to be withdrawn by either the buyer or seller upon proper written notice to the bank.

135. Under what circumstance may a broker deposit his or her own money into an escrow account?

    1. Never; the broker may not commingle funds.
    2. After securing written permission from the Pennsylvania Real Estate Commission
    3. To maintain a minimum balance required by the bank
    4. If the buyer's earnest money check was returned due to insufficient funds

136. During a listing presentation, a prospective seller informs the salesperson of his intent to refuse to sell the property to persons of a specific national origin group. What is the best course of action for the salesperson in this situation?

    1. List the property and follow the instructions of the seller as is required under the law of agency
    2. List the property but document the conversation in the listing file with reference to company policy of nondiscrimination
    3. Refuse to list the property for sale if the seller persists in his intention to discriminate because of the national origin of a buyer prospect
    4. Refuse to accept a written exclusive listing on the property but agree to represent the seller under an oral open-listing agreement

137. A professional businessperson who is a member of a minority group wants to rent space in a commercial office building managed by a broker. The broker quotes the prospect a higher rental rate than is quoted to nonminority prospects considering the same space. Which of the following statements is *TRUE?*

    1. By presenting different terms based on the prospect's minority status, the broker has violated both federal and state fair housing laws.
    2. Although the broker's action is not a violation of federal fair housing laws, it is a violation of the Pennsylvania Human Relations Act.
    3. Neither federal nor state law covers discriminatory conduct involving a commercial office property.
    4. The broker's license cannot be suspended or revoked by the Pennsylvania Real Estate Commission because the broker has not violated the license law.

138. What are the consequences when a real estate salesperson is found guilty of violating any provision of the Pennsylvania Human Relations Act?

    1. The Pennsylvania Human Relations Commission may suspend or revoke the salesperson's license.
    2. The employing broker is liable for the conduct of the salesperson, so the employing broker will also be guilty of the violation.
    3. The Pennsylvania Human Relations Commission will notify the state Real Estate Commission of findings of violations against licensees under the Pennsylvania Human Relations Act.
    4. The Pennsylvania Human Relations Commission must refer the case to HUD for prosecution under the appropriate federal law.

139. A 55-year-old individual inquires about renting a three-bedroom, single-family home that a broker has listed for rent. In response to this inquiry, which of the following actions by the broker is legal?

    1. Refusing to show the property to the prospect because the owner has instructed the broker to rent only to people under the age of 40
    2. Informing the prospect that the owner would accept less than the stated security deposit because the property would only be occupied by one person
    3. Charging a rental amount different from what would be charged to a family with children
    4. Verifying income and ordering a credit check in order to determine the applicant's ability to meet his or her obligations under the terms of the lease

140. A housing discrimination charge must be filed with the Pennsylvania Human Relations Commission within

    1. six months.
    2. one year.
    3. two years.
    4. 30 days.

141. A landlord has a "no pets" policy in her apartment building. A trainer or handler of guide dogs for persons with disabilities wants to rent an apartment from the landlord and requests that guide dogs be permitted in the apartment. Does the landlord have to let the dog in?

    1. If the landlord's "no pets" policy is applied uniformly in a nondiscriminatory manner, it may be legally applied to guide dogs as well.
    2. The Pennsylvania Human Relations Act specifically prohibits the landlord from refusing to rent to the handler or trainer of guide or support animals on the basis of the owner's "no pets" policy.
    3. Under the Pennsylvania Human Relations Act, the landlord may not discriminate against the visually impaired person on the basis of a "no pets" policy, but the landlord may require the tenant to pay an additional security deposit or charge a higher rental rate.
    4. The Pennsylvania Human Relations Act does not address the issue of guide, hearing, or support dogs or other animals.

142. A Pennsylvania real estate salesperson may lawfully collect compensation for engaging in real estate activities from

    1. either a buyer or a seller.
    2. his or her employing broker only.
    3. any party to the transaction or the party's representative.
    4. a licensed real estate broker who cooperated with the salesperson's employing broker.

143. A licensed salesperson may hold an active license with more than one Pennsylvania broker under which of the following circumstances?

    1. Under no circumstances
    2. With the permission of his or her sales manager
    3. With the written consent of the brokers being represented
    4. With the permission of the Pennsylvania Real Estate Commission

144. When a sole proprietor broker has his or her license suspended for two years, what effect does this have on the associate brokers and salespeople affiliated with the broker?

    1. Affiliates' licenses will be revoked, subject to reinstatement after one year.
    2. Affiliates' licenses will also be suspended for a two-year period.
    3. Suspension has no effect on the affiliates.
    4. Affiliates' licenses are terminated.

145. Once issued, a salesperson's license must be

    1. carried by the salesperson at all times.
    2. maintained at the main office of the employing broker.
    3. displayed in a conspicuous place at the local association of REALTORS®.
    4. presented to the consumer prior to engaging in an initial interview with the consumer.

146. When a salesperson applies for a real estate license, the employing broker is responsible for

    1. issuing an official transcript verifying completion of the educational requirement.
    2. submission of a sworn statement certifying that she will actively train and supervise the applicant.
    3. verifying that the candidate is a U.S. citizen.
    4. payment of the initial fee to the Real Estate Recovery Fund on behalf of the licensee.

147. A licensed salesperson may perform all of the following activities for or on behalf of his employing broker EXCEPT

    1. negotiate a loan on real estate.
    2. lease commercial office space.
    3. buy or offer to buy real estate.
    4. appraise a single-family property.

148. If an employing broker refuses to pay compensation to one of his or her licensees according to the terms of an employment contract, the licensee may

    1. immediately file an application for compensation from the Real Estate Recovery Fund.
    2. transfer all of her current listings to a new employing broker.
    3. petition the Pennsylvania Real Estate Commission to arbitrate the dispute.
    4. file a lawsuit against the broker.

149. Which of the following is *TRUE* of a real estate salesperson's license?

    1. It must be shown to every consumer at the initial interview.
    2. It is issued in the name of the salesperson exclusively and may be used to represent more than one broker at the same time.
    3. It is not valid until the broker certifies that the salesperson has completed the company training program.
    4. It must be maintained with the current license of the broker at the main office of the broker.

150. When the employing broker submits a salesperson's license application to the Pennsylvania Real Estate Commission, the broker is certifying that the

    1. salesperson is a citizen of the United States.
    2. salesperson has not been convicted of any criminal offense.
    3. broker will actively supervise and train the salesperson.
    4. salesperson has successfully completed the mandatory education requirement.

151. A broker intends to open a branch office in a neighboring town. The broker applies for a branch office license under the same name as the main office. The broker names a licensed real estate salesperson as the branch office manager. In this situation, will the broker receive approval for the branch office?

    1. Yes, the broker has fully complied with the requirements of the license law.
    2. No, under the license law, brokers cannot have branch offices operating under the same name in more than one municipality.
    3. Yes, the broker is in compliance with the requirement that a broker may directly control and supervise only one office or branch by naming a salesperson as the branch manager.
    4. No, the manager of a branch office must be a licensed real estate broker or associate broker.

152. A broker who maintains multiple branch offices wants to give an associate broker managing a branch office authority to directly hire salespeople or other associate brokers. Is this permitted?

    1. Yes, provided that a list of all licensees employed by the branch office manager is maintained at the main office of the employing broker
    2. No, only the broker is authorized to hire or employ salespeople or associate brokers
    3. No, only the broker of record may supervise and direct activities in branch offices that he or she maintains
    4. Yes, if the associate broker managing the office is a partner or corporate officer of the broker

153. What are the procedures that a salesperson must follow when he or she decides to terminate the affiliation with an employing broker and affiliate with a different broker?

    1. Give the broker an official letter of termination that the broker may send to the Pennsylvania Real Estate Commission
    2. Do nothing; the employing broker is responsible for notifying the Pennsylvania Real Estate Commission of the change
    3. Return all transaction records and prospect leads to the employing broker
    4. Return his or her license with the properly completed change of employer form and payment of the required fee

154. An associate broker is not satisfied with her present real estate company and has decided to change employing brokers. Before the associate broker may begin actively selling for the new company

    1. the first broker must transfer the associate broker's license to the new office.
    2. the new employing broker must notify the Commission of the change, pay the required fee, and send in the proper forms before the associate broker may perform any activities on behalf of the new employing broker.
    3. the associate broker must take her current license to the new brokerage and notify the Commission within three days of the transfer to a new location.
    4. the associate broker must notify the Commission no later than ten days after the intended date of change, pay the required fee, and return her current license to the Commission.

155. When a licensed broker changes his or her place of business, all of the following are true *EXCEPT*

    1. the Commission will issue a new license immediately because the broker is already licensed.
    2. the broker's license may be suspended or revoked if the Commission is not notified of the change.
    3. all licensees registered at that location must make application to the Commission for a current license at the new location.
    4. the new office location must comply with the terms of the license law.

156. An associate broker is changing employing brokers. While the change of employment forms are being processed by the Commission, the associate broker may

    1. represent both employing brokers until the new license is received.
    2. manage a branch office on behalf of the new employing broker.
    3. continue to list properties for sale in the name of the former employing broker.
    4. act as a transaction licensee without representing either broker until the new license is processed.

157. In Pennsylvania, an exclusive-right-to-buy contract

    1. is illegal.
    2. may run for an indefinite period of time.
    3. must be indicated as such in the buyer agency agreement.
    4. requires the signature of the principal only.

158. In Pennsylvania, representation agreements that obligate the buyer to pay a fee

    1. must be in writing.
    2. must be on specific forms approved by the Real Estate Commission.
    3. are not regulated under the license law.
    4. are not permitted; only sellers pay fees for real estate services.

159. All of the following provisions are included in the Pennsylvania Real Estate Commission's rules regarding exclusive listing agreements *EXCEPT*

    1. a listing agreement must state the fee the broker expects to earn.
    2. a listing agreement must be accompanied by a qualified expert's report of the property's condition.
    3. an exclusive listing agreement must be in writing and signed by the seller.
    4. the seller must receive a copy of the listing agreement after signing it.

160. All of the following must appear in a written exclusive listing agreement *EXCEPT*

    1. the commission or fee to be received by the broker.
    2. a complete legal description of the property being sold.
    3. the time duration of the listing.
    4. the proposed gross sales price of the property.

161. A broker signs a three-month listing agreement with a seller. The agreement contains the following clause: "If the property has not been sold after three months from the date of this signing, this agreement will automatically continue for additional three-month periods thereafter until the property is sold." In Pennsylvania, this clause is

    1. legal because it contains a reference to a specific time limit.
    2. illegal.
    3. illegal if there are more than three renewal periods.
    4. legal because the renewal periods are for less than one year.

162. Certain topics must be included in exclusive listing agreements or the licensee may face disciplinary action. All of the following must be included in the listing agreement *EXCEPT*

    1. the specified commission rate or amount.
    2. the specific termination date.
    3. the broker protection clause.
    4. the asking price.

163. Upon obtaining an exclusive listing, a broker or licensed salesperson is obligated to

    1. set up a listing file and issue it a number in compliance with Pennsylvania Real Estate Commission Rules and Regulations.
    2. place advertisements in the local newspapers.
    3. cooperate with every real estate office wishing to participate in the marketing of the listed property.
    4. give the person or persons signing the listing a legible, signed, true, and correct copy.

164. Which type of listing agreement would be required to contain a statement in boldfaced type stating that the broker earns a commission on the sale of property during the listing period even if the owner sees the property without the aid of the broker?

    1. Exclusive-right-to-sell listing
    2. Exclusive agency listing
    3. Multiple listing
    4. Open listing

165. A broker lists a commercial property for sale. The listing

    1. is required to be an exclusive-right-to-sell contract.
    2. must include a cancellation notice to terminate the contract after the original term.
    3. is exempt from requirements governing disclosures regarding the Real Estate Recovery Fund.
    4. must state that payments of money received by the broker on account of a sale shall be held by the broker in escrow pending consummation or termination of the transaction.

166. A property owner will be leaving the state for at least a year. She lists the property with a broker on an exclusive-right-to-sell basis for a term of six months. Which of the following should be included in the listing contract?

    1. Automatic renewal clause in case the property does not sell during the original six-month period
    2. Language authorizing the broker to execute a signed agreement of sale on behalf of the owner
    3. Specific language requiring a cancellation notice to terminate the listing agreement at the end of the six-month listing period
    4. Statement in boldfaced type that the broker earns a commission on the sale of the property during the listing period no matter who made the sale, including the owner

167. An agreement between a rental listing referral agent and a prospective tenant must include

    1. an itemized list of charges payable to the rental listing referral agent.
    2. a guarantee that the purchaser will find a satisfactory rental unit through the service.
    3. the rental specifications desired by the prospective tenant, such as location and rent.
    4. a disclosure that the rental listing referral agent will act as the agent of the lessee when negotiating lease terms.

168. A licensed salesperson may prepare a comparative market analysis when the

    1. mortgage lender contracts with the salesperson to perform the analysis for a mortgage loan application.
    2. property owner requests the analysis for purposes of appealing a property tax assessment.
    3. salesperson is attempting to secure a listing agreement from an unrepresented seller.
    4. salesperson has completed a required course on the Uniform Standards of Professional Appraisal Practice.

169. A salesperson is discussing the possibility of listing a seller's home for sale. Before the agreement is signed, the salesperson should provide the seller with information concerning

    1. the broker's policies regarding cooperation with other brokers, including the sharing of fees.
    2. the common or typical rate of commission charged by brokers in the area.
    3. the approximate number of times the house will be advertised for sale.
    4. the inclusion of an automatic renewal clause in the broker's exclusive listing agreement.

170. Under certain circumstances, which of the following agreements may be oral?

    1. Exclusive agency listing
    2. Open listing
    3. Exclusive-right-to-sell
    4. Exclusive buyer agency

171. A property owner wants to list his property for sale with a broker but does not want to sign an exclusive listing contract. May the broker accept an oral open listing?

    1. Yes, as long as the licensee provides the seller a written memorandum stating the terms of the agreement
    2. No, Commission rules require that all contracts and agreements be in writing.
    3. No, the statute of frauds requires that listing agreements be in writing in order to be enforceable.
    4. Yes, as long as the parties agree that the licensee is not acting as an agent of the seller in the transaction

172. What type of listing agreement would require the broker to provide the seller with a written memorandum stating the terms of the agreement?

    1. Multiple listing shared among several brokers
    2. Exclusive agency listing
    3. Exclusive-right-to-sell listing
    4. Oral open listing

173. When must a licensee provide statements of estimated costs to parties involved in the purchase of real estate?

    1. One business day prior to closing the transaction
    2. When the buyer makes formal application for a mortgage loan
    3. Before an agreement of sale is executed
    4. At the closing when title is passed from the seller to the buyer

174. How accurate are statements of estimated cost and return provided by licensees required to be?

    1. As accurate as may be reasonably expected of a person having knowledge of and experience in real estate sales
    2. Within 10 percent of the actual figures determined at settlement
    3. Because they are only estimates, there is no specific requirement regarding accuracy of the information provided.
    4. The statements provided must be within $500 of the actual cost or return in order to avoid liability.

175. When a licensee provides a statement of estimated cost and return to parties involved in a transaction, the statements

    1. may be provided orally to the parties.
    2. must be provided on standard forms developed by the Pennsylvania Real Estate Commission.
    3. are not required if a lender agrees to provide the statement at the loan application.
    4. must be provided in writing before an agreement of sale is executed between the parties.

176. Failure to include which of the following in an agreement of sale would give a buyer the option to void the agreement without a requirement of court action?

    1. Zoning classification of the property if the agreement is for a commercial building
    2. Mortgage contingency if the buyer is securing financing
    3. Specific date for possession and closing
    4. Complete and accurate legal description of the property

177. If an agreement of sale is conditioned on the ability of the buyer to obtain mortgage financing, all of the following must be included in the agreement *EXCEPT*

    1. the deadline for the buyer to obtain the mortgage loan.
    2. a copy of the buyer's credit report.
    3. the nature and extent of assistance that the broker will render to the buyer.
    4. the type of mortgage.

178. Regarding agreements of sale, all of the following statements are true *EXCEPT*

    1. the licensee must furnish a copy of the sales contract to all signatories at the time of execution.
    2. the licensee must retain copies in his or her files for three years from the date it was signed.
    3. the agreement must contain a statement identifying the capacity in which the broker is engaged.
    4. the agreement must contain a statement that access to a public road may require issuance of a highway occupancy permit.

179. When are statements of estimated cost and return provided to the parties to a transaction by the broker involved in the transaction?

    1. Before an agreement of sale is executed by the parties
    2. One business day prior to settlement of the transaction
    3. Within three days of the buyer's loan application
    4. When all contingencies addressed in the contract have been satisfied

180. Statements of estimated costs and returns must

    1. be signed by the seller and buyer upon receipt.
    2. be an exact representation of all costs to be incurred by the party for whom they were prepared.
    3. be presented to the parties prior to execution of an agreement of sale.
    4. include a disclosure indicating who the broker that prepared the statements represents.

181. When a broker negotiates an agreement of sale between a buyer and seller, the broker is responsible for all of the following *EXCEPT*

    1. furnishing a copy of the agreement of sale to both parties at the time of execution.
    2. furnishing a copy of the agreement with original signatures of all parties to the mortgage lender.
    3. preserving a copy of the agreement for a period of three years following its consummation.
    4. ensuring that the agreement of sale is in writing.

182. When included as a provision in an agreement of sale, a mortgage contingency must include all of the following *EXCEPT*

    1. type of mortgage.
    2. maximum interest rate of the mortgage.
    3. amount of the mortgage payment.
    4. deadline for the buyer to obtain the mortgage.

183. All of the following are mandatory provisions of a sales contract *EXCEPT*

    1. identifying the rate or amount of commission to be paid to the broker.
    2. identifying the capacity in which the broker is engaged in the transaction.
    3. describing the purpose of the Real Estate Recovery Fund.
    4. a statement of the zoning classification of the property, except in cases where the property is zoned solely or primarily to permit single-family dwellings.

184. Which of the following provisions must be included in an agreement of sale?

    1. Dates for payment and conveyance
    2. Language relieving the seller of responsibility for defects discovered after settlement
    3. Zoning classification for single-family housing
    4. Language addressing the buyer's ability to secure mortgage financing

185. Which of the following is a mandatory provision in an agreement of sale negotiated by a broker between a buyer and seller?

    1. Earnest money deposit to be held by the listing broker
    2. Payment of the brokerage commission
    3. Dates for payment and conveyance
    4. Zoning classification in the case of residential property sales

186. If a broker receives money belonging to another under an installment land purchase agreement, the transaction is considered consummated when

    1. the buyer has been afforded the opportunity to record the agreement, unless the agreement specifies otherwise.
    2. legal title passes from the seller to the buyer.
    3. all terms of the installment agreement have been satisfied.
    4. the parties sign the installment land purchase agreement.

187. An aggrieved person is awarded a judgment against a real estate licensee for violation of the Real Estate License and Registration Act. Regarding the recovery fund, the aggrieved party

    1. may immediately apply to the Commission for payment from the recovery fund for the full judgment amount plus court costs and attorney fees.
    2. has the right to a maximum award amount of $20,000 from the recovery fund.
    3. may seek additional money from the licensee in a private civil action after being compensated from the recovery fund.
    4. may seek a $10,000 maximum recovery from the recovery fund plus limited court costs and attorney fees.

188. A broker is found guilty of fraud or misrepresentation and ordered to pay monetary damages to a consumer. What is the time frame within which the injured party may file a claim for payment from the Real Estate Recovery Fund?

    1. One year after the alleged violation occurred
    2. One year after termination of the proceedings in connection with the judgment awarded to the consumer
    3. Three years after the alleged violation occurred
    4. Three years after the date on which a professional relationship of trust and accountability commenced between the broker and the consumer

189. The maximum compensation that will be paid from the Real Estate Recovery Fund to satisfy claims against a licensee is

    1. $5,000.
    2. $10,000.
    3. $25,000.
    4. $100,000.

190. Whenever the Commission is required to satisfy a claim against a licensee with money from the Real Estate Recovery Fund, the licensee

    1. may continue engaging in real estate activities under the Commission's direct supervision.
    2. must repay the full amount plus interest to the account for his or her license to be reinstated.
    3. may expect the Pennsylvania Real Estate Commission to foreclose on any property owned by the licensee.
    4. must agree to a monthly payment schedule in order to maintain an active license.

191. At what point may the Commission assess an additional fee against each licensee in order to add to the amount of money in the recovery fund?

    1. If, at the beginning of a biennial renewal period, the balance in the fund is less than $300,000
    2. At any point when the amount available in the fund is below $500,000
    3. When the Commission is directed to do so by executive order of the governor
    4. At any regularly scheduled Commission meeting

192. When the court orders a payment to be made from the recovery fund owing to the improper activities of a licensee, what happens to the licensee?

    1. The license is automatically suspended as of the date of payment.
    2. The Pennsylvania Real Estate Commission takes no further action against the licensee.
    3. The licensee's license is automatically revoked.
    4. The licensee is subject to a fine of up to $1,000 but maintains an active license.

193. Which of the following statements about the Real Estate Recovery Fund is *TRUE*?

  1. A buyer may apply directly to the fund to cover the cost of repairs to the property necessary because the licensee failed to disclose a defect.
  2. An agreement of sale must contain disclosure language advising the parties of the existence of the fund with a phone number to call for complete details.
  3. All brokers and salesperson licensees pay an assessment of $10 at each renewal period to fund the recovery fund.
  4. Brokers may apply to the fund for payment of referral fees from out-of-state brokers.

194. When a person obtains a final judgment against a licensee and seeks payment from the Real Estate Recovery Fund, what is the time frame for making application for payment from the fund?

  1. Within six months of the date of the violation that resulted in the judgment being issued
  2. No more than one year after the termination of the proceedings, including reviews and appeals, in connection with the judgment
  3. Application must be received by the Commission within 30 days of the initial decision of the court directing the licensee to pay compensation.
  4. Application may be made at any time after termination of the proceeding, because no specific time frame is provided by law.

195. All of the following are true regarding the Real Estate Recovery Fund *EXCEPT*

  1. the recovery fund does not apply to the sale of campground memberships.
  2. a licensee on whose behalf money has been paid must reimburse the fund plus interest at 10 percent per year.
  3. a licensee on whose behalf money has been paid will have his or her license automatically suspended as of the date of payment.
  4. the maximum liability of the fund may not exceed $20,000 for any one claim.

196. In addition to all other fees, any person receiving an initial license may pay how much into the Real Estate Recovery Fund?

  1. $5
  2. $10
  3. $25
  4. $64

197. The Pennsylvania Real Estate Commission may assess an additional fee against licensees in order to increase the balance in the Real Estate Recovery Fund if

  1. during any one year, the amount paid from the fund exceeds $500,000.
  2. the number of new license fees during a biennial renewal period drops below $25,000.
  3. the Department of State determines that available funds appear insufficient to satisfy outstanding claims.
  4. at the beginning of a biennial renewal period, the balance in the fund is less than $300,000.

198. The purpose of the Real Estate Recovery Fund is to

    1. provide a direct source of compensation to sellers if the broker mishandles escrow deposits.
    2. enable the public to secure payment of uncollected judgments against licensees.
    3. provide a source of funds to settle disputes between buyers and sellers arising from agreements of sale.
    4. compensate real estate salespeople if a salesperson's employing broker declares bankruptcy.

199. A residential borrower whose loan is in default but whose property has not yet been sold at a foreclosure sale has certain rights. Under the equitable right of redemption in Pennsylvania, the borrower

    1. must always pay the full outstanding balance due plus attorney fees and costs to avoid foreclosure.
    2. loses all property rights when the lender exercises its right under the acceleration clause and initiates the foreclosure proceeding.
    3. may cure the default and avoid the foreclosure sale by bringing the payments up-to-date if the outstanding balance is $50,000 or less.
    4. must wait until the sale before offering to make any payments.

200. A commercial office building sold for $1 million. The buyer paid $400,000 as a down payment and secured a $600,000 first mortgage loan. How much is the Pennsylvania state transfer tax?

    1. $4,000
    2. $6,000
    3. $10,000
    4. $20,000

201. In Pennsylvania, certain deed transfers are exempt from the transfer tax. However, a tax will have to be paid on a transfer

    1. between parent and child.
    2. between government bodies.
    3. between educational institutions.
    4. of unimproved land to a developer.

202. Under the Pennsylvania mechanic's lien law, the claim

    1. must be filed by the contractor or subcontractor within four months after the work is completed.
    2. becomes a general, involuntary lien against the property.
    3. may only be filed by the general contractor hired by the property owner.
    4. may be filed only with permission from the property owner.

203. All of the following will provide protection against the possibility of mechanics' liens being filed against property by subcontractors *EXCEPT*

    1. mechanic's lien insurance.
    2. waiver of liens in a construction contract.
    3. stipulation against liens filed at the prothonotary's office.
    4. release of liens document.

204. A nonlicensed owner of a multifamily investment property collects a security deposit of $500 from each tenant entering into a one-year lease. The security deposit funds

    1. must be held in an escrow account in a federally or state-regulated banking or savings institution.
    2. must be immediately deposited in an interest-bearing account with the interest payable to the tenant at the end of the year.
    3. may be retained in the owner's personal checking or savings account used to cover business expenses related to the building.
    4. are not regulated because the owner does not hold a real estate license.

205. The maximum amount that landlords may require a residential tenant to pay as a security deposit in the first year of the lease is an amount

    1. not to exceed one month's rent.
    2. equivalent to two months' rent.
    3. one-half of one month's rent.
    4. agreed to by the landlord and tenant.

206. According to the Pennsylvania statute of frauds, which of the following agreements must be in writing in order to be enforceable?

    1. Two-year lease for an apartment in a multifamily building
    2. Commercial lease for a five-year term
    3. One-year commercial lease negotiated by a broker representing the building owner
    4. Month-to-month residential lease

207. The primary purpose of public meetings held by the Real Estate Commission is to

    1. inform licensees about changes in Commission policies.
    2. solicit from members of the public their suggestions, comments, and objections about real estate practice in Pennsylvania.
    3. conduct disciplinary proceedings involving licensees in a forum and manner available to members of the public.
    4. allow special interest groups and professional organizations to influence Commission rulemaking.

208. Which of the following licensees is *NOT* required to satisfy mandatory continuing education requirements to renew the license?

    1. An individual licensed as a rental listing referral agent
    2. A licensed broker acting as broker of record for a corporation holding a broker's license
    3. An associate broker employed to teach prelicensing real estate classes at a community college
    4. An individual holding a salesperson's license who assists a broker in managing commercial properties

209. An advertisement by a licensee that offers prizes, certificates, or gifts may contain all of the following *EXCEPT*

    1. a description of each prize, certificate, or gift offered.
    2. the fair market value of each prize, certificate, or gift offered.
    3. the odds of winning or receiving each prize, certificate, or gift.
    4. the location of the office at which the prize, certificate, or gift may be claimed.

210. In a cooperating broker transaction, when the seller is represented by a listing broker and the buyer is represented by a broker acting as a buyer's agent, which broker holds the buyer's earnest money deposit in an escrow account?

    1. The listing broker always has the duty to hold the earnest money deposit on behalf of the seller.
    2. The broker representing the buyer is required to hold the buyer's earnest money deposit.
    3. With appropriate notices to buyer and seller, either broker may assume the duty to hold the earnest money deposit in an escrow account.
    4. Because of the conflict of interests, the earnest money deposit should be held by a disinterested third party.

211. Which of the following statements is *TRUE* concerning a salesperson licensee who is convicted of a felony or misdemeanor while holding an active salesperson's license?

    1. The licensee must notify the Commission of the conviction within 30 days of the verdict.
    2. The licensee is only required to notify the Commission if the offense involved activities related to acts for which a real estate license is required.
    3. The salesperson's license is automatically suspended if the individual is convicted of a felony or misdemeanor.
    4. The employing broker of the salesperson licensee is responsible for notifying the Commission and recommending appropriate disciplinary action.

212. Which of the following is a requirement for relicensure of an individual whose license has been revoked by the Commission?

    1. The individual is not permitted to reapply for licensure for a period of at least ten years after revocation.
    2. If relicensure is permitted by the Commission, the individual must comply with all current requirements for licensure before the license is issued.
    3. The individual must provide certifications from at least three people attesting to the individual's honesty, integrity, and competency.
    4. The individual must complete 14 hours of mandatory continuing education prior to the license's being reissued.

213. May a licensed real estate salesperson collect a referral fee for construction, repair, or inspection services utilized by a consumer as a result of the licensee's referral?

    1. Yes, if the licensee provides the consumer with a written disclosure of the referral fee or commission at the time the licensee first advises the consumer that the service is available or when the licensee first learns the consumer will be using the service
    2. Yes, but only if the licensed salesperson is also an owner or employee of the firm providing the construction, repair, or inspection service
    3. No, because the real estate licensee may never receive compensation from anyone other than the employing broker
    4. No, because the consumer is required to independently select providers of services related to the real estate transaction

214. All of the following are purposes and goals of mandatory continuing education programs required for license renewal *EXCEPT*

    1. maintaining and increasing competency to engage in licensed real estate activities.
    2. keeping a licensee abreast of changes in laws, regulations, practices, and procedures that affect the real estate business.
    3. better ensuring that the public is protected from incompetent practice by licensees.
    4. ensuring a revenue stream to the Real Estate Commission that enables it to conduct educational and regulatory activities.

215. A broker acting as a transaction licensee would be in violation of the Real Estate Commission's rules and regulations if the broker engaged in which of the following activities?

    1. Providing assistance with document preparation
    2. Advising the consumer about compliance with laws pertaining to real estate transactions without rendering legal advice
    3. Disclosing to a buyer that the seller will accept a price less than the asking/listing price
    4. Keeping the consumer informed about the transaction and the tasks to be completed

216. Which of the following is a requirement of the Commission regarding an escrow account maintained by a licensed Pennsylvania real estate broker?

    1. The account must be used exclusively for deposits of earnest money deposits and rental payments being held on behalf of a consumer.
    2. The account must be maintained in a federally insured bank, savings association, or credit union.
    3. The account must provide for withdrawal of funds without prior notice.
    4. The account must designate the broker or licensed employee of the broker as trustee.

217. If the Real Estate Commission receives a copy of a complaint filed with the Pennsylvania Human Relations Commission alleging that a licensee has violated a provision of the Pennsylvania Human Relations Act, what is the waiting period before the Real Estate Commission may proceed with its own disciplinary action against the licensee?

    1. 90 days if it is an initial complaint against the licensee
    2. One year
    3. The Real Estate Commission may not act until after the Pennsylvania Human Relations Commission has decided the case.
    4. There is no waiting period. Both the Real Estate Commission and Pennsylvania Human Relations Commission must begin investigations immediately upon receipt of a complaint.

218. Which of the following individuals is *NOT* required to hold a real estate license when engaging in real estate activities?

    1. An individual employed full-time by a builder-owner of single-family homes who is authorized to sell homes owned by the builder-owner employer
    2. A person acting as a trustee in bankruptcy proceedings
    3. An individual acting as an independent contractor who sells or offers to sell campground memberships
    4. A person who owns or manages a business that collects rental information for the purpose of referring prospective tenants to rental units

219. Licensing fees required under the Real Estate Licensing and Registration Act are fixed by which of the following?

    1. The Professional Licensure Committee of the state House of Representatives
    2. The Department of State
    3. The Appropriations Committee of the state Senate
    4. The state Real Estate Commission

220. Which of the following requirements must be met in order for an individual to be issued a real estate license?

    1. The individual must have a reputation for honesty, trustworthiness, integrity, and competence to transact business.
    2. The individual must be a U.S. citizen.
    3. The individual must certify that he or she has not been convicted of a felony or misdemeanor within the three years immediately preceding application for licensure.
    4. The individual must be financially solvent and have an acceptable credit rating.

221. If a licensed salesperson or associate broker desires to change his or her employment from one licensed broker to another, what is required in order for the licensee to conduct activities on behalf of the new employing broker?

    1. The salesperson or associate broker may not engage in any activity on behalf of the new employing broker until a new license is received from the Real Estate Commission.
    2. The salesperson or associated broker must notify the Commission in writing no later than ten days after the intended date of change, pay the required fee, and return his or her current license.
    3. The previous employing broker and prospective employing broker must agree to the license transfer before the Commission will issue the new license.
    4. The salesperson or associate broker must provide a current state police criminal record check with the application for license transfer.

222. If a seller provides inaccurate or incomplete information on a property condition disclosure statement, is the licensee liable for the action of the seller?

   1. Yes, because the licensee has a responsibility to conduct an independent inspection of the property
   2. No, because the licensee has no duty to conduct an independent inspection or verify the accuracy of statements reasonably believed to be accurate and reliable
   3. Yes, because the licensee must verify the accuracy of any representations made by the seller-client on a disclosure statement
   4. No, because the licensee is not a party who would be harmed as a result of the inaccurate or incomplete information

223. Which of the following may be given written authority to withdraw funds from a broker's escrow account for payments properly chargeable to the account?

   1. An unlicensed accountant or bookkeeper employed by the broker
   2. A member of the Real Estate Commission conducting an investigation of the brokerage company
   3. A licensed salesperson employed by the broker designated as trustee for the account
   4. An unlicensed clerical or administrative employee acting on behalf of the employing broker

224. An agreement between a broker and consumer in which the consumer is committed to pay a fee must be in writing, signed by the consumer, and contain all of the following information *EXCEPT*

   1. a statement describing the purpose of the Real Estate Recovery Fund and phone number of the Commission at which information regarding the fund may be obtained.
   2. a statement describing the nature and extent of the broker's services to be provided to the consumer.
   3. a statement identifying any possibility that the broker may provide services to more than one consumer in a single transaction.
   4. a statement authorizing the broker to designate a licensee employed by the broker to act as the sole and exclusive agent of the consumer.

225. Under what circumstance may a real estate licensee perform a comparative market analysis for a consumer?

   1. A licensee may perform a comparative market analysis for a seller-client only after the licensee and seller have entered into an exclusive listing agreement.
   2. A licensee representing a seller-client may prepare a comparative market analysis for an unrepresented buyer in order to assist the buyer in determining an offering price.
   3. A licensee may perform a comparative market analysis only if he or she is an unbiased, disinterested third party, acting with impartiality and independence.
   4. A licensee under contract to act as a buyer's agent may perform a comparative market analysis for the purpose of determining the offering price for a specific parcel of real estate in an identified market at a specified time.

A N S W E R   K E Y

1. (1) The broker has fulfilled her obligation under the terms of the listing contract with the seller by procuring a ready, willing, and able buyer and is therefore entitled to recover her agreed-upon compensation. She may not sue the buyer and may not retain the deposit as compensation.

2. (4) Brokerage fees are established solely as a result of a negotiated agreement between the broker and the consumer. The broker is required to disclose this to the consumer at the initial interview (608(8)). Fees are not determined by law, the Real Estate Commission, or local brokers.

3. (1) Brokerage fees are established by agreement between the broker and the consumer to whom the broker provides service. The broker may not share these fees with an unlicensed individual (604(a)(12.1)). The broker must maintain the earnest money deposit until the transaction is consummated or terminated.

4. (4) License law prohibits a salesperson or associate broker from accepting a commission or any valuable consideration for the performance of any act specified in the law from any person except the licensed real estate broker with whom he or she is affiliated (604(a)(12)).

5. (4) The licensed salesperson and employing broker agree to the terms of compensation to be paid by the broker to the salesperson. Professional organizations, multiple listing services, and other parties, such as sellers, do not dictate or control compensation arrangements.

6. (4) In Pennsylvania, dual agency is permitted if both parties give their fully informed consent in writing (606.4(a)).

7. (2) The original agent may not disclose offers received during the first listing. The fiduciary duty of confidentiality continues after the termination of the agency relationship (606.1(g)). The agent is not a dual agent, because the original agent no longer has an agency relationship with the seller.

8. (3) The agent should not gain information about motivation and urgency, which is generally of a confidential nature and should not be discussed outside of an agency relationship. The agent may provide information on properties for sale in the area, discuss mortgage interest rates and terms, and discuss various levels of representation available to the buyer.

9. (3) Written consent to act as a dual agent must include a statement of the terms of compensation (606.4). Both parties must consent to the dual compensation. Neither must be represented by attorneys, nor do they have to be related.

10. (1) The seller must consent in writing in order for the listing broker to extend an offer of subagency (606.1(c)). The cooperating broker acting as a subagent must provide the consumer notice and appropriate documentation to the buyer prospect (606.1(b)(4)). The buyer is not the one to agree to the offer of subagency.

11. (3) By entering into an agency agreement with a prospective tenant, the broker assumes full fiduciary responsibilities without regard for the issue of compensation. The broker has not operated in a manner consistent with the best interest of his client.

12. (1) The salesperson has failed to comply with the state law. Prior to engaging in a substantive discussion, the licensee is required to provide the consumer with a consumer notice disclosing information required by law (608).

13. (1) In a dual agency situation, the licensee owes certain fiduciary duties to both parties. Simply providing comparable market data about recent sales to the buyer does not compromise the duties owed to the seller and would therefore not be a violation of the agent's duty under the law of agency.

14. (4) The agent's duty of confidentiality continues after termination of the agency relationship. Information gained during the original agency relationship may not be revealed or used by the licensee for the benefit of the licensee or a third party (606.1(g)).

15. (2) The licensee should disclose a professional opinion of value and recommend that the property be listed at market value. A licensee is expected to exercise reasonable professional skill and care when dealing with the public and to deal honestly and in good faith (606.1(a)).

16. (2) Agency relationships may be created either orally or in writing. A written agreement is necessary when the broker is providing a service for a fee. Brokers may represent buyers and sellers in the same transaction with written consent from both parties (606.1(b)).

17. (2) Explaining contract terms may be construed as practicing law. Real estate licensees are not permitted to practice law unless they are licensed attorneys-at-law. One of the duties of licensees when working with consumers is to advise the consumer to seek expert advice on matters related to the transaction that are beyond the licensee's expertise (606.1(a)(8)).

18. (3) The salesperson has violated license law and ethical business practices that prohibit inducing a party to break a contract for the purpose of substituting a new one when such substitution is motivated by the personal gain of the licensee (604(a)(11)).

19. (2) A licensed broker supervising the termination of a deceased broker's business may continue to promote existing listings unless otherwise directed by the seller but may not enter into new listing agreements or hire new licensees. Pending contracts may continue until consummation (35.252(b)).

20. (3) The consumer must be provided with the Consumer Notice at the initial interview. The best evidence is the buyer's signature on the form, but a licensee may provide a service without the buyer's actually signing the document. The licensee, however, must retain appropriate documentation that the Consumer Notice was provided.

21. (4) The licensee must disclose in writing the licensee's intention or true position if the licensee purchases any property that has been listed with his or her office (604(a)(13)).

22. (1) The Consumer Notice must be provided to a purchaser/tenant at the initial interview, which is defined as the first contact where a substantive discussion about real estate needs occurs (608).

23. (4) A broker is permitted to act as a dual agent provided the broker secures the written consent of both parties to the transaction. The requirement is informed consent after full disclosure as provided at the initial interview (606.4(a)).

24. (1) A licensee who sells or leases his or her own real estate must disclose this licensure in advertisements for the property. This requirement does not apply if the property is listed for sale with a real estate company (35.304).

25. (3) During the initial interview, the licensee must provide a Consumer Notice containing disclosures required by the rules of the Commission (608). An initial interview is considered the first contact between a licensee and a consumer where a substantive discussion of real estate needs occurs.

26. (2) A salesperson who is selling or leasing his or her own real estate is required to disclose licensed status to a prospective buyer or lessee before an agreement is entered into. Rents are not deposited into an escrow account. Only the employing broker may compensate a licensed salesperson employed by that broker (35.288).

27. (4) The broker must disclose his license status prior to entering into an agreement with an owner (35.332(c)). A broker may not incorporate an option to purchase property in a listing agreement for the property, and the broker may not conduct business through a straw party.

28. (2) The salesperson's failure to provide the Consumer Notice at the initial interview is a violation of the license law (604(a)(15.1)). Licensees are subject to disciplinary action by the Commission, including possible suspension or license revocation.

29. (3) A property condition disclosure form is not required in the sale of commercial property. A disclosure is required even if a licensee is not involved (for sale by owner) by an absentee owner and if the buyer was a tenant in the property.

30. (1) Pennsylvania law requires the seller to provide the buyer with the property condition disclosure statement prior to the buyer's entering into an agreement of sale with the seller.

31. (4) The property condition disclosure requirements pertain to most residential transactions and cover a broad range of issues affecting the property. The licensee should advise the seller of the disclosure requirements and the seller's obligation to comply with requirements of the statute.

32. (1) The buyer may sue both the seller and broker who both have legal liability for disclosing a material defect that was known to them and not made known to the buyer prospect.

33. (4) Sale of a two-unit property owned by a licensee and sold for sale by owner is not one of the exempt transactions, so the seller must make appropriate disclosures. The Real Estate Seller Disclosure Act provides for nine instances in which disclosure requirements do not apply: new construction covered by a builder's warranty, foreclosure sale, and conveyance between one spouse and another.

34. (3) The Real Estate Seller Disclosure Act requires property condition and defects to be disclosed to the prospective buyer. The current statute does not require disclosure of a situation like the suicide of the former seller.

35. (3) There is currently no statutory requirement addressing the disclosure of the murder. Federal fair housing laws prohibit any discussion of AIDS or HIV. Licensees must be aware of potential legal liability that could arise in this situation and should seek guidance from legal counsel.

36. (1) Each member of the Pennsylvania Real Estate Commission is appointed by the governor (202(a)). The members are not selected by REALTORS® or elected by the public or real estate licensees.

37. (2) The governor appoints members to the state Real Estate Commission (202(a)). No endorsement from any professional organization is required, nor is there any requirement regarding posting a surety bond. Salesperson licensees are not qualified to serve on the Commission.

38. (4) The state Real Estate Commission must include five members who are, at the time of appointment, licensed and qualified brokers under the existing law (202).

39. (1) Members of the Real Estate Commission are appointed by the governor (202(a)), not the state Association of REALTORS®. The Commission prescribes subjects for testing, but the department contracts with a professional testing service to write and administer exams (403). The Commission also promulgates rules and regulations (404) and reports to legislative committees (408).

40. (2) The Pennsylvania Real Estate Commission has the power and authority to administer and enforce the license law (406). The Pennsylvania Association of REALTORS® is a trade association whose members are licensees. The Department of Housing and Urban Development generally handles fair housing, not licensing issues.

41. (4) The purpose of laws, including licensing laws, is to provide for the good, safety, and welfare of the public. The rationale supporting the validity of the law is the government's responsibility to ensure that the public is protected.

42. (1) The Pennsylvania Real Estate Commission administers and enforces laws governing the conduct of licensees (404). The state legislature enacts laws that govern licensees. The Department of State arranges for the services of a professional testing service to write and administer examinations (403).

43. (2) The Commission may not investigate a random selection of licensees. The Pennsylvania Real Estate Commission may commence an investigation of a licensee's conduct upon its own motion as well as upon receipt of a verified complaint in writing from a consumer (604).

44. (1) There is no provision in the Commission rules for interviewing consumers or members of the public (35.246(d)). The Commission or its authorized representative may interview the broker as well as other licensed or unlicensed employees who work in the office.

45. (4) The Pennsylvania Real Estate Commission does not have statutory authority to issue licenses. Licenses are issued by the Department of State (401). The Commission prescribes subjects to be tested (403), approves schools (402), and may waive continuing education requirements (404.1).

46. (4) Campground membership salespeople are required to be licensed and are subject to disciplinary action on the part of the Commission (581). Appraisal firms are regulated by the state Board of Certified Real Estate Appraisers rather than by the Pennsylvania Real Estate Commission. Officers of banking institutions and attorneys-in-fact are excluded from the license law (304).

47. (1) License law provides that the employing broker might not be liable for a violation committed by a licensee employed by the broker. If the broker had actual knowledge, or if the licensee engaged in a course of dealing that the broker should have been aware of, liability could accrue to the employing broker (702(a)(c)).

48. (1) It is legal for a broker to recruit salespeople or associate brokers employed by competitors. Violations of the license law include placing a For Sale sign without written consent of the seller, failing to specify a definite termination date, and failing to exercise adequate supervision of a licensee's activities (604(a)(8)).

49. (4) Antitrust laws are enforced by federal and state agencies other than the Pennsylvania Real Estate Commission, but the license law, rules of the Commission, and state fair housing laws are all topics addressed by license law as grounds for disciplinary action against licensees by the Commission.

50. (2) License law prohibits a licensed broker from paying compensation to anyone other than his or her licensed employees or another broker, and it prohibits a salesperson from accepting compensation from anyone other than his or her employing broker (604(a)(12)).

51. (2) License law specifically prohibits a broker from paying a commission or other valuable consideration to anyone other than his or her licensed employees or another real estate broker (604(a)(12.1)).

52. (2) A licensee is required to notify the Commission of being convicted, pleading guilty, or *nolo contendere* to a felony or misdemeanor within 30 days of the verdict or fee (35.290(a)). Being convicted in a court of competent jurisdiction in Pennsylvania or any other state could result in suspension or revocation of the broker's license (604(a)(14)).

53. (3) As a result of a hearing, the Commission may decide to suspend or revoke a license as well as impose fines not exceeding $1,000 (604(a)). The Commission has no authority to imprison a licensee. The Department of State, not the Pennsylvania Real Estate Commission, issues real estate licenses (401).

54. (3) The Commission may suspend or revoke a license or impose a fine of up to $1,000, or do both, if a licensee is found guilty of making any substantial misrepresentation. The Commission does not have authority to impose a jail sentence (604(a)).

55. (2) License law provides that any person who engages in business without being licensed is subject to criminal prosecution. The first offense is a summary offense punishable by a fine not exceeding $500, imprisonment not exceeding three months, or both (303).

56. (1) The maximum penalty would be a fine of $5,000 and imprisonment for a period of two years. Specifically, the penalty for conviction for a second or subsequent offense is a fine of not less than $2,000 but not more than $5,000, imprisonment for not less than one year but not more than two years, or both (303).

57. (4) A broker's compensation is negotiable between the parties. Misleading advertising is prohibited under 604(a)(5), and being convicted of a felony could result in revocation of the broker's license under 604(a)(14).

58. (2) The broker is required to deposit earnest money into an escrow account. Erecting a For Sale sign without written consent is a violation of 604(a)(8), and the issue of honesty and competency is addressed under 604(a)(20).

59. (4) While the conduct addressed in each choice could cause a license to be suspended, the only issue that requires an automatic suspension of the license is when the Commission pays money from the recovery fund to settle a claim against a licensee (803(f)).

60. (2) A broker may place a For Sale sign on a property after receiving permission to do so. Brokers may not engage in discriminatory conduct (604(a)(22)). Only the broker has authority and responsibility to escrow funds in connection with real estate transactions (35.325(a)). Advertisements regarding prizes must state the prerequisites for receiving the prize or gift (35.306(a)(2)).

61. (4) Salespeople and associate brokers are employed by and provide services on behalf of their employing broker. If the broker's license is suspended or revoked, licenses of the associate brokers and salespeople are terminated. To remain in active practice, the affiliates are required to find new employing brokers.

62. (2) License law provides that the broker may have his or her license suspended or revoked only if the broker had actual knowledge of the violation (702(b)) or if the conduct of the salesperson demonstrated a course of dealing that could serve as *prima facia* evidence of knowledge on the part of the broker (702(c)).

63. (2) Any person whose license has been revoked may reapply at the end of a five-year period from the date of revocation. The applicant must meet all of the licensing qualifications of the act, including the examination requirement (501(c)).

64. (1) A common course of dealing followed by an employee constitutes *prima facia* evidence of knowledge upon the part of the employing broker and could result in suspension or revocation of the brokers license (702(c)).

65. (1) The broker must obtain the written consent of the owner before erecting a For Sale or For Rent sign on property (35.301(a); 604(a)(8)). The broker does not have to gain permission from the neighbors or local governing body, or sell the property. It is permissible to have signs on open listings as well as on exclusives. Written consent, however, is always required.

66. (3) An advertisement by a salesperson must contain the business name and phone number of the employing broker (35.305(b)). Real estate salespeople may not advertise under their own names.

67. (2) All licensees are required to disclose their license status in advertisements for property if the property is not listed for sale with a real estate company (35.304).

68. (2) Advertisements by a broker about production or position in the market must identify the municipality that the market comprises (35.307(b)).

69. (3) The business name of the broker as designated on the license must be included in all advertising (35.305). The phone number of the broker must be included if the advertisement includes the name and phone number of a salesperson or associate broker.

70. (3) A broker is required to advertise under the business name designated on the license (35.305). The listing price or name of the listing salesperson is not required in advertising. A disclosure notice must be provided at the initial interview with a consumer.

71. (1) The Real Estate Commission policy regarding Internet advertising requires that the broker's name as it appears on the license must be included on each page of the site on which the firm's advertisement occurs. The broker does not have to include license numbers, lists of licensees, or their addresses and phone numbers.

72. (2) Any advertisement, including Web site advertising, must include the business name of the broker as it appears on the license. Recently adopted Commission policies require that the broker's name and phone number be included on each page of Web site advertising.

73. (4) License law prohibits the filing of any suit or action claiming compensation for any act for which a license is required if the person filing suit was not duly licensed at the time of offering to perform such act or service (302).

74. (1) Upon conviction for a first offense for practicing real estate without a license, the maximum penalty is a fine not exceeding $500, imprisonment not exceeding three months, or both (303).

75. (1) Owners of real estate conducting business with respect to their own property are not required to be licensed. They are excluded from licensure (304(1)).

76. (4) The unlicensed person may do nothing. An unlicensed salesperson is involved in illegal activity and has no recourse to recover compensation (302).

77. (3) In the case of a corporation or partnership, this exclusion shall not extend to more than five of its partners or officers (304(1)). The provisions of the license law do not apply to owners conducting business with regard to their own property.

78. (1) An individual directly employed by the owner of multifamily residential property for the purpose of managing or maintaining the property is exempt from provisions of the license law. So long as the owner retains the authority to make decisions, the employee may show apartments and provide information on rentals. Unlicensed employees may not negotiate terms or conditions, nor may they enter into leases on behalf of the owner (304(10)).

79. (4) An attorney-at-law who receives a fee for rendering services within the scope of an attorney-client relationship is exempt from licensure (35.302(5)) and so may handle the transaction. As an owner, the corporation may designate no more than five of the corporation's officers to act on behalf of the corporation as the owner.

80. (3) This person has no recourse. License law prohibits the filing of suits seeking recovery for conduct engaged in, in violation of the license law. The terms *consultant, counselor, agent,* or *finder* are all directly included in the definition of a broker (201).

81. (3) Any person who remains inactive for a period of five years without renewing his or her license must, prior to having a license reissued, take and pass the examination pertinent to the license for which the person is reapplying (501 (b)). There is no education or training requirement as a condition to reactivating a license on inactive status for more than five years.

82. (4) Rules governing offices do not prohibit a licensed broker from employing salespeople or associate brokers when the broker's office is located in a private residence. The rules do provide that the office must have a separate entrance, that the business name be displayed, and that the office allow for business to be conducted privately (35.342).

83. (1) Managing real estate is an activity included in the definition of a real estate broker provided in the license law, so a company will need a license (201). Licensed attorneys, partnerships acting as owners of property, and resident managers employed by owners of multifamily residential properties are excluded from the license law (304).

84. (1) Corporations, partnerships, and associations can be issued a broker's license if the individual designated as the broker of record meets the individual requirements to be issued a broker's license. The Real Estate Commission processes license applications. Employees engaging in the real estate business may hold a salesperson's, rather than broker's, license. Each individual is required to pay a fee to the recovery fund (513 and 802).

85. (4) Sections 521 and 522 establish requirements, which include that the application must be received by the Commission within three years of the date on which the applicant passed the examination. Qualifications for licensure as a salesperson do not include college education or a minimum age of 21. Conviction for a felony offense does not preclude the applicant from being issued a license.

86. (2) An individual who undertakes to promote the sale, exchange, purchase, or rental of real estate or who represents himself or herself to be a real estate consultant, counselor, agent, or finder is required to hold a broker's license (201(1)). A for sale by owner or for rent by owner is exempt, as is a resident manager and a licensed auctioneer at a bona fide auction.

87. (4) The education requirement for a salesperson is completion of 60 hours of real estate instruction in areas of study prescribed by the Commission (521). Citizenship is not a requirement for licensure nor is a degree from a college or university.

88. (1) Unlicensed individuals directly employed by an owner of residential multifamily buildings for the purpose of managing or maintaining the property are not required to be licensed, but the scope of activities they may perform is limited. They may show apartments, provide information on rental amounts, and explain building rules and regulations (304(10)). Unlicensed individuals may not prepare and enter into leases, negotiate terms or conditions, or hold money belonging to tenants.

89. (4) The applicant for licensure as a broker in Pennsylvania is required to have been engaged as a licensed real estate salesperson or possess educational or experience qualifications that the Commission deems to be the equivalent thereof (511(4)). Residency or posting of a performance bond are not required of a broker candidate. The applicant must be a high school graduate or provide proof of an education equivalent thereto (511(2)).

90. (4) The application must be received by the Commission within three years of the date of passing the license exam (512(c)). Neither citizenship nor a college degree is required of broker candidates. Qualifying experience is not limited to the field of real estate sales; a candidate could qualify for licensure with other experience.

91. (1) A builder-owner salesperson applicant must take and pass the salesperson's examination but has no mandatory education requirement (551). Campground membership and cemetery salesperson applicants have no examination requirement. Rental listing referral applicants have both an education and an examination requirement.

92. (3) There is no examination or coursework required for a cemetery salesperson. Builder-owner salespeople (551), rental listing referral agents (561), and cemetery brokers (531) are all required to pass a written exam prior to licensure.

93. (3) There is no education requirement or exam required for a cemetery salesperson (541). Campground membership salespeople (581), time-share salespeople (591), and rental listing referral agents (561) are all required to complete education or training requirements as a condition of licensure.

94. (1) An individual who wants to take the broker's examination must be a high school graduate or have passed a high school general equivalency exam (35.271(a)). There is no residency requirement, and candidates may possess education or experience that the Commission considers equivalent to three years' experience as a licensed salesperson. Recommendations are required for licensure as a broker rather than as a condition of taking the examination.

95. (3) The requirements for mandatory continuing education requirements apply to real estate brokers and real estate salespeople only. They do not apply to other activities for which licenses are required (i.e., time-shares, cemetery brokers, or licensed builder-owners) (404.1(a)).

96. (2) All licenses expire at the end of the license period established by the Commission. Salesperson and broker licenses all expire the last day of May in even-numbered years and must be renewed on or before June 1.

97. (4) Commission rules (35.382) require a broker or salesperson to complete 14 hours of Commission-approved continuing education as a condition precedent to renewal of a current license. Renewal fees established by the Commission must also be paid (407(a)). There is no requirement to be actively participating in the real estate business, nor must the licensee be a Pennsylvania resident.

98. (2) Appraisal activities are regulated by the state Board of Certified Real Estate Appraisers rather than by the Pennsylvania Real Estate Commission. A broker may manage real estate, do a comparative market analysis, and be a real estate consultant or counselor.

99. (2) Negotiating the sale of real estate for another in return for a fee is a license-required activity. Residential multifamily property managers who are employed directly by the owner, persons holding power of attorney, and owners conducting real estate business with regard to their own property are excluded from the license law (304).

100. (3) Any persons employed by an owner for the purpose of managing or maintaining multifamily residential property are excluded under the license law with regard to certain activities they may perform (304(10)). Collecting rents in this situation would not be an activity requiring licensure.

101. (4) It is illegal to engage in any activity for which a license is required until the license has actually been issued by the state. Completing the requirements for licensure and processing paperwork to the state does not mean that a candidate is licensed.

102. (1) Real estate licensees are not authorized to engage in appraisal activities. Appraisal activities are regulated by the state Board of Certified Real Estate Appraisers. The other activities are permitted under the definition of a salesperson in the license law (201) and rules of the Commission (35.201).

103. (1) A real estate license is not required for the sale of business opportunities. Upon passing the license exam, a candidate is qualified to apply for a license. Until the license is issued by the state, an individual may not engage in any activity for which a license is required. Such activities include holding open houses for the public, preparing comparative market analyses, and negotiating loans on real estate.

104. (2) A rental listing referral agent is defined as an individual or entity that owns or manages a business that collects rental information for the purpose of referring prospective tenants to rental units or locations of rental units (201 and 35.201). Rental listing referral agents are not authorized to show rental units, collect fees or security deposits, or engage in property management activities.

105. (1) A builder-owner salesperson is a full-time employee of a builder-owner of single-family and multifamily dwellings who is authorized to list for sale, sell, lease, or rent any real estate owned by his builder-owner employer (201).

106. (1) A time-share salesperson's license is required to sell time-shares (201). Employees of a public utility, trustees in bankruptcy, and licensed auctioneers are all exempt from licensing requirements (304).

107. (2) The broker of record is the individual broker responsible for the real estate transactions of a licensed partnership, association, or corporation (35.201).

108. (3) Only licensed employees of the broker may hold open houses for the public and withdraw funds from the broker's escrow account. Personal assistants may be employed by either the broker or salesperson to perform secretarial and clerical duties without being licensed.

109. (3) License law prohibits a licensee from accepting a commission or any valuable consideration for the performance of any act specified in the act from anyone except the licensed real estate broker with whom he or she is affiliated (604 (a)(12)).

110. (1) An individual holding a salesperson's license issued by another jurisdiction must prove that this license has been active within five years prior to submission of the application. The applicant is required to pass only the Pennsylvania portion of the license exam. It is possible to hold active licenses in more than one state simultaneously, and residency is not a requirement for licensure (35.223(b)).

111. (1) License law prohibits a licensee from accepting compensation from anyone other than her employing broker (604(a)(12)).

112. (3) The nondisclosure is a violation of the law. License law (606.1(a)(13)) requires licensees to disclose to the consumer any financial interest (including referral fees) derived from services to be provided to the consumer by any other person, including inspection services

113. (4) The broker may thank the airline pilot. Brokers are prohibited from sharing fees with or paying compensation to an unlicensed person (604(a)(12.1)).

114. (3) A purchaser has the right to cancel the purchase of a time-share interest until midnight of the fifth day following the date on which the purchaser executed the purchase contract (609(a)).

115. (3) A purchaser has the right to cancel a time-share purchase until midnight of the fifth day following the date on which the purchaser executed the purchase contract (609(a)). Any promotional prizes or gifts issued to the purchaser remain the property of the purchaser (609(d)).

116. (2) Brokers and salespeople may fill in the blanks of preprinted contract forms but may not engage in the practice of law. Advising parties on the significance or consequence of contract terms is engaging in the practice of law and should be avoided. The broker is a special agent hired with limited authority that ordinarily does not extend to binding principals to a contract.

117. (1) Opinions regarding condition of title to the property being sold could constitute the practice of law and should be avoided. Mandatory requirements and disclosures are addressed in the law (608.2(1)), requirements regarding estimates of cost and return are addressed in 35.334, and records must be maintained for three years (604(a)(6)).

118. (4) A broker is responsible for depositing money into the escrow account by the end of the next business day following its receipt, unless both the buyer and the seller have given written permission for the broker to refrain from depositing the money pending the seller's acceptance of the offer (35.324(a) and 35.324(b)).

119. (2) Brokers are required to maintain a separate custodial or escrow account separate from any business or personal account. The broker is required to keep records of all funds deposited into the account. There is no requirement to maintain a separate account for each deposit (35.325 and 604(a)(5)).

120. (1) License law requires the broker to immediately deposit earnest money deposits into a separate custodial or trust fund account maintained by a bank or recognized depository until the transaction is consummated or terminated (604(a)(5)(iv)).

121. (4) Salespeople and associate brokers who receive deposits or other moneys related to a transaction in which they are engaged on behalf of a broker-employer are required to promptly pay the deposit to the broker (604(a)(5)). The broker is required to maintain an escrow account.

122. (2) Brokers must maintain records of transactions for three years following consummation of the transaction. There is neither a requirement addressing number of employees nor a requirement that a licensee affiliate with any professional organization.

123. (2) License law requires the broker to keep records relating to a real estate transaction for three years following consummation of the transaction (604(a)(6)).

124. (2) License law requires disclosure to the consumer of any interest a licensee has in any services to be provided to the consumer by any other person, including construction or repair services. (606.1(a)(13)). Failure to make the disclosure could result in disciplinary action against the licensee (604(a)(19)).

125. (2) Commission rules prohibit a broker from commingling money required to be held in escrow with business, personal, or other funds. However, a broker is permitted to deposit business or personal funds to cover service charges or maintain minimum balance requirements of the institution (35.326(b)).

126. (1) License law provides that a broker involved in property management activities on behalf of a lessor be required to maintain a separate rental management account for such deposits (604(a)(5)). The broker should not deposit rents in either an escrow account or the broker's general business account.

127. (1) The employing broker may give a licensed employee written authority to withdraw funds from the escrow account (35.325(b)) and may give an unlicensed employee written authority to deposit money into an escrow account.

128. (3) In cooperating broker transactions, the duty to escrow funds can be the responsibility of either broker. Rules of the Commission provide that if the buyer gives the deposit to the listing broker rather than to the selling broker, the listing broker assumes the escrow duty (35.323(a)). All parties must have a full disclosure as to which broker is holding the deposit in escrow.

129. (3) Commission rules require the broker to provide a letter authorizing the release of records pertaining to the escrow account (35.325(d)). A broker's escrow account is required to designate the broker as trustee. If money is expected to be held in escrow for more than six months, the broker is encouraged to deposit the money into an interest-bearing escrow account. The general,

recognized practice is that escrow accounts do not bear interest. Rents must be deposited in a rental management account maintained by the broker, not in the broker's escrow account.

130. (2) If a dispute arises, the broker retains the escrow until the dispute is resolved (35.327). A broker's duty to escrow may not be waived or altered by agreement between the parties to the transaction, between the broker and the parties, or between the broker and other brokers involved in the transaction (35.322). If the money is expected to be held in escrow for more than six months, the broker is encouraged to deposit the money into an interest-bearing account. However, most escrow accounts do not bear interest.

131. (4) Rules of the Commission provide that the broker is responsible for depositing money into an escrow account by the end of the next business day following its receipt in the office where the escrow records are maintained. However, if the money is in the form of a check under an offer to purchase, the broker may, with the written consent of both buyer and seller, refrain from depositing the check pending the sellers' acceptance of the offer (35.324(b)).

132. (1) Any interest earned is held and disbursed pro rata in the same manner as the principal unless the parties agree otherwise (35.325(c)). Brokers may deposit funds in escrow accounts earning interest, and they are encouraged to do so if money is expected to be held in escrow for more than six months.

133. (3) If an earnest money deposit is in the form of a check accompanying an offer to purchase, a broker may, with the written permission of both the buyer and seller, refrain from depositing the check pending the seller's acceptance of the offer (35.324(b)).

134. (3) The broker must maintain an escrow account at a bank or recognized depository designating the broker as trustee. The broker is responsible for holding the escrow deposit pending consummation or termination of the transaction (35.321 and 35.325).

135. (3) Rules of the Commission permit a licensed broker to deposit personal funds into an escrow account to cover service charges assessed by the bank or to maintain a minimum balance as required by the bank (35.326(b)).

136. (3) Both license law and fair housing law make it illegal for a broker to accept any listing on the understanding that illegal discrimination in the sale or rental of housing will be practiced. Accepting a listing on such conditions subjects the licensee to possible disciplinary action by both the Pennsylvania Real Estate Commission and the Pennsylvania Human Relations Commission (604(a)(22)).

137. (2) A broker who discriminates against a prospect in either commercial or residential property transactions is in violation of both the Pennsylvania Human Relations Act and the license law. The Pennsylvania Human Relations Act differs from federal fair housing law in that it covers both residential and commercial properties.

138. (3) Actions of the Human Relations Commission finding licensees guilty require notification to the state Real Estate Commission (604(a)(22)). The Pennsylvania Human Relations Commission does not have the power to suspend or revoke licenses. Although the salesperson may be guilty, the employing broker is not always liable.

139. (4) Verification of income and credit checks to determine the applicant's ability to meet financial obligations are legal and do not constitute discriminatory conduct. The broker may not refuse to rent based on the prospect's age. Anyone over the age of 40 constitutes a protected class in

Pennsylvania. The landlord may not discriminate based on age by different rental terms, such as security deposits or rental amounts.

140. (2) The Pennsylvania Human Relations Commission applies the same standards provided for in federal law (i.e., complaints must be filed within one year of the alleged violation).

141. (2) The Pennsylvania Human Relations Act specifically prohibits discrimination against handlers or trainers of guide or support animals as well as persons with disabilities who use guide or support animals. Any violation of the Pennsylvania Human Relations Act also constitutes a violation of the license law (604(a)(22)).

142. (2) License law prohibits a salesperson or associate broker from accepting compensation from anyone other than his or her employing broker (604(a)(12)).

143. (1) Under no circumstances may a licensed salesperson act on behalf of two employing brokers at the same time. No licensed salesperson may be employed by any other broker than is designated upon the current license issued to the salesperson.

144. (4) Salespeople and associate brokers are employed by and provide services on behalf of their employing broker. If the broker's license is suspended or revoked, licenses of the associate brokers and salespeople are terminated. To remain in active practice, the affiliates are required to find new employing brokers.

145. (2) Commission rules require that the current license of all licensees employed by or affiliated with the broker shall be maintained at the main office of the broker (35.245(a)). There is no requirement that the actual license be carried by the salesperson, that it be presented to consumers, or that it be prominently displayed.

146. (2) Rules of the Commission require that the salesperson's license application include a sworn statement from the employing broker certifying that the broker will actively train and supervise the applicant (35.223(2)(i)). Education providers issue transcripts, not employing brokers. Citizenship is not a requirement for licensure. Fees paid to the recovery fund are the responsibility of the applicant rather than of the employing broker.

147. (4) The definition of a salesperson does not allow a licensed salesperson to engage in appraisal activity (201). It does allow the salesperson to list for sale, sell or offer for sale, buy or offer to buy, or to negotiate the purchase sale or exchange of real estate and to negotiate a loan, lease, rent, or offer to lease or rent or place for rent any real estate.

148. (4) Disputes between an employing broker and salesperson employed by the broker are contract issues to be settled in a court of law. The Commission does not arbitrate such disputes. Listings are not the property of the salesperson and cannot be unilaterally transferred to a new broker, and the recovery fund is not available until all court action has been concluded.

149. (4) The current license of the broker and all licensees employed by or affiliated with that broker must be maintained at the main office of the broker (35.245(a)). The license is issued to the salesperson in order for him or her to provide service on behalf of the employing broker only. There is no requirement that it be provided to consumers.

150. (3) In order to be licensed as a salesperson, the candidate must submit a license application with a sworn statement from the broker certifying that the broker will actively supervise and train the applicant (35.223(a)).

151. (4) License law requires that each branch office be under the direction and supervision of a manager who is either the broker or an associate broker (601(b)). A salesperson may not manage a licensed branch office.

152. (2) Only the broker has the authority by the license law to hire or employ salespeople or associate brokers. Although a branch office may be under the direction and supervision of a manager who is an associate broker, the associate broker does not have authority to directly hire or employ other licensees (603(a)).

153. (4) License law stipulates that when a licensed salesperson desires to change employing brokers, the salesperson must notify the Commission in writing, pay the required fee, and return his or her current license (603(a)).

154. (4) When licensees change employing brokers, they are required to notify the Commission in writing no later than ten days after the intended date of change, pay the required fee, and return their current license. The associate broker maintains a copy of the notification sent to the Commission as a temporary license pending receipt of the new current license (603(a)).

155. (1) The broker is required to maintain a fixed office, which is required to meet standards prescribed by the Commission (35.242). Should the broker decide to move the location of a licensed office, license law requires the new location to be approved and licensed, and all licensees registered at the former location must make application for a new license at the new location (601(a)).

156. (2) The associate broker may manage a branch office on behalf of the broker. When an associate broker changes employment from one broker to another, he or she may, in the interim when the new license is being processed, maintain a copy of the notification sent to the Commission as a temporary license pending receipt of the new license (603(a)).

157. (3) Section 606.1(b)(1) requires the nature of the service to be provided must be set forth in a written agreement between the consumer and the licensee. Section 608.1 establishes requirements for the written agreement. An exclusive-right-to-buy contract must be in writing and contain a specific termination date.

158. (1) Section 608.1 establishes that any agreement between a broker and a principal, whereby the consumer is obligated to pay a fee, must be in writing and signed by the consumer. This includes brokerage agreements: seller listing and buyer representation.

159. (2) A qualified expert's report covering property condition is not required when a seller lists property for sale with a broker. In most transactions, state law requires the seller to complete a property condition disclosure form prior to entering into an agreement of sale. The listing must state the broker's fees, be in writing, and be signed by the seller, who must receive a copy of the listing after signing it.

160. (2) A listing contract is not required to specify the complete legal description of the property being sold. Mandatory provisions of exclusive listing contracts are established by Real Estate Commission regulation 35.332. Exclusive listing contracts are required to contain the sale price, the commission expected, and the duration of the agreement.

161. (2) This clause is illegal in Pennsylvania because Commission rules and regulations prohibit the use of automatic renewal clauses in exclusive listing agreements (35.332(c)(2)).

162. (3) A broker may or may not include a broker protection clause; that issue is not addressed by license law. The law requires that a definite termination date be included in an exclusive listing (604(a)(10)). Rules of the Commission require that the asking price and a specified commission rate or amount be included in an exclusive listing agreement.

163. (4) License law requires the licensee to furnish a copy of the listing to all signatories at the time of execution (604(a)(9)). Although brokers normally set up a listing file, advertise properties, and cooperate with other brokers, none of these activities is required by rule or statute.

164. (1) Commission rules require that an exclusive-right-to-sell listing must include specific language in boldfaced type that the owner will be obligated to pay the brokerage fee even if the owner sells the property without the aid of the broker (35.332(a)(4)).

165. (4) A commercial listing must state that money received by the broker will be held by the broker in escrow pending consummation or termination of the transaction (35.331). All listings must contain information about the existence of the recovery fund. There is no requirement that a commercial listing be an exclusive-right-to-sell contract. The broker may not require notification to terminate the listing. Requirements governing inclusions and exclusions in listing agreements cover both residential and commercial property listings without distinction.

166. (4) Exclusive-right-to-sell listing contracts are required to contain a statement in boldfaced type that the broker earns a commission on the sale of the property during the listing period, no matter who made the sale, including the owner (35.332(b)). An exclusive listing may not contain an automatic renewal clause or language giving the broker authority to execute an agreement of sale. The broker may not require a cancellation notice to terminate the listing at the end of the six-month period (35.332(c)).

167. (3) An agreement between a rental listing referral agent and a prospective tenant must contain the rental specifications desired by the tenant, such as location and rent (35.335). The only function of the rental listing referral agent is to furnish the prospective tenant with lists of available rental units.

168. (3) A comparative market analysis may be performed for the purpose of determining the offering price for property when a salesperson is securing a listing agreement with the seller (201 and 608.3).

169. (1) When an initial interview takes place prior to entering into a listing, the broker must provide information about the broker's policy regarding cooperation with other brokers (608(6)). Commission rates are not determined by local custom. Automatic renewal clauses are prohibited (35.332(c)).

170. (2) A licensee may enter into an oral open listing agreement if he or she provides the seller or lessor with a written memorandum stating the terms of the agreement (35.281(b)).

171. (1) Commission rules provide for oral open listings with sellers provided certain conditions are met (35.281(b)). Oral open listings may be used to create an agency relationship. The statute of frauds does not apply to listing contracts.

172. (4) A licensee who enters into an oral open listing agreement must give the seller a written memorandum stating the terms of the agreement (35.281(b)).

173. (3) A real estate licensee is required to provide each party with a written estimate of reasonably foreseeable expenses associated with the sale before an agreement of sale is executed (35.334(a)).

174. (1) Rules of the Commission require that the estimates of costs required to be provided to the parties be as accurate as may reasonably be expected of a person having knowledge of and experience in real estate (35.334(b)).

175. (4) Rules of the Commission require the licensee to provide written estimates of reasonably foreseeable expenses before an agreement of sale is executed (35.334(a)). The disclosure must be made in writing on forms developed for such purpose. The Commission does not mandate a standard form. Lenders provide statements to prospective borrowers rather than to both parties involved in the transaction.

176. (1) Although all four options may be important issues to address in an agreement of sale, Commission rules specifically address the issue of the zoning classification. The zoning classification, unless the property is zoned for single-family housing, must be included or the buyer has the option of voiding the agreement with no requirement of court action (35.333(a)(6)).

177. (2) There is no requirement that a buyer include a copy of his of her credit report with an offer to purchase property. Commission rules specify what must be included if an agreement of sale is conditioned on the ability of the buyer to obtain mortgage financing (35.333(b)). These include a deadline for the buyer to obtain the loan commitment, assistance that the broker will provide the buyer, and the type of mortgage.

178. (2) The broker is required to keep records relating to real estate transactions for three years following consummation or termination of the transaction. Mandatory inclusions in agreements of sale include the following: copy of sales contract given to signatories, statement regarding broker's services, and statement that access to a public road may require obtaining a highway occupancy permit: statute 608.2 and Commission rule 35.333.

179. (1) The broker must provide each party with a written estimate of reasonably foreseeable expenses associated with the sale that the party may be expected to pay before an agreement of sale is executed (35.334(a)).

180. (3) Statements of cost and return must be presented prior to entering into an agreement of sale. They are expected to be as accurate as may be reasonably expected of a person having knowledge of real estate sales. There is no requirement for signatures or disclosures of agency representation (35.334).

181. (2) There is no requirement for the broker to deliver copies to a mortgage lender. Licensees are responsible for ensuring that contracts are in writing (35.281(a)), that copies are preserved for a period of three years (604(a)(6)), and that a copy of the agreement is presented to all signatories (604(a)(9)).

182. (3) The amount of the mortgage payment is not included in mortgage contingency clauses (35.333(b)). If an agreement of sale is conditioned upon the ability of the buyer to obtain a mortgage, the agreement must contain the type of mortgage, the maximum interest rate, and the deadline for obtaining the mortgage.

183. (1) There is no statutory or regulatory requirement for the rate or amount of the broker's compensation to be disclosed in an agreement of sale. Mandatory provisions of an agreement of sale include disclosure to the parties regarding the role of the broker, the existence of the Real Estate Recovery Fund, and the zoning classification of property (608.2).

184. (1) Rules of the Commission provide that an agreement of sale must contain the dates for payment and conveyance in addition to other specified items. Language addressing the seller's responsibility for

defects, zoning classification of single-family property, and mortgage financing language are not mandatory inclusions (35.333).

185. (3) Date for payments and conveyance must be addressed in the contract (35.333(a)). Earnest money deposits are not required as part of an agreement of sale. The broker's commission is not an issue in an agreement of sale between a buyer and seller. Zoning classification must be provided in the case of properties other than those zoned for residential use.

186. (1) Commission rules provide that if the broker receives money belonging to another under an installment land purchase agreement, the transaction will be considered consummated when the buyer has been afforded the opportunity to record the agreement, unless the contract provides otherwise.

187. (2) When an aggrieved person obtains a final judgment against a licensee, the aggrieved party may file an application for payment from the Real Estate Recovery Fund. The maximum payment from the fund is $20,000 for any one claim (803(d)).

188. (2) A claim for payment from the recovery fund must be made no more than one year after the termination of the proceedings, including reviews and appeals in connection with the judgment (803(b)(4)).

189. (4) The liability of the recovery fund may not exceed $20,000 for any one claim and may not exceed $100,000 per licensee (803(d)).

190. (2) If the Commission pays an amount in settlement of a claim against a licensee, the license of that person is automatically suspended upon the effective date of payment and will not be reinstated until the licensee has repaid the amount in full plus interest at the rate of 10 percent per year (803(f)).

191. (1) If, at the beginning of any biennial renewal period, the balance in the fund is less than $300,000, the Commission may assess an additional fee against each licensee, up to a maximum of $10, in order to bring the balance in the fund up to $500,000 (802).

192. (1) The license is automatically suspended as of the effective date of payment when payment is made from the recovery fund. In order for the licensee to have the license reinstated, the licensee must repay the full amount plus interest at the rate of 10 percent per year (803(f)).

193. (2) Commission rules provide that every agreement of sale must contain specific language regarding the existence of the recovery fund (35.333(a)(9)). The recovery fund is available to consumers only after they have secured a final judgment against a licensee. Licensees do not pay fees at each renewal; they are assessed an amount to be paid at the time of original license application.

194. (2) License law provides that an aggrieved person who has been awarded a judgment by a court of competent jurisdiction must make application to the recovery fund no more than one year after the termination of the proceedings, including reviews and appeals (803(b)(4)).

195. (2) There is no requirement that the money must be repaid. It must be repaid in order to reinstate a license. If money is paid from the recovery fund on behalf of a licensee, the license of that person will automatically be suspended as of the effective date of payment. No such license will be reinstated until the licensee has repaid the money in full plus interest at the rate of 10 percent per year (803(f)).

196. (2) Every licensee is required to pay $10 into the Real Estate Recovery Fund at the time of his or her initial license application (802).

197. (4) The Commission may reassess each licensee an amount not to exceed $10 if, at the commencement of a biennial renewal period, the balance in the recovery fund is less than $300,000 (802).

198. (2) The Real Estate Recovery Fund was created to provide a vehicle by which consumers who have obtained a final judgment against a licensee may recover compensation from the Commission. Application to the fund may be made only after all reasonable remedies available have been exhausted (803).

199. (3) In Pennsylvania, a borrower may cure default in a residential mortgage loan with an outstanding balance of $50,000 or less by merely bringing the payments up-to-date rather than by paying the entire outstanding debt. This may be done after default but before the foreclosure sale.

200. (3) On a $1 million sale, the state transfer tax is $10,000 ($1,000,000 × 1%). The Pennsylvania Realty Transfer Tax is 1 percent of the full sale price. In addition, Pennsylvania law permits the local taxing districts to impose an additional transfer tax.

201. (4) A transfer of unimproved land is subject to transfer taxes. The state tax is 1 percent of the full consideration paid for the property, and the local taxing bodies can levy an additional tax on the transfer. Transfers between parents and children or among siblings, between government bodies, or between charitable, religious, or educational institutions are exempt from transfer taxes.

202. (1) Generally, the mechanic's lien law requires the contractor or subcontractor to file a claim with the court of common pleas in the county in which the property is located within four months after the work is completed. If successful, the lien is a specific, involuntary lien, which may be claimed without the consent of the property owner.

203. (2) A waiver of liens in a construction contract protects the title from liens being filed by the general contractor, not subcontractors. A recorded stipulation against liens, a release of liens document, and mechanic's lien insurance can all be used as a means of protecting the property against claims of subcontractors or suppliers.

204. (1) Pennsylvania law requires landlords to hold security deposits in an escrow account that must be in a federally or state-regulated banking or savings institution. The tenant must be notified of the name and address of the institution where the deposits are held. Interest-bearing accounts are not required until the second anniversary of the lease.

205. (2) Pennsylvania law limits the amount landlords may charge as a security deposit. During the first year of tenancy, the maximum is an amount equal to two months' rent. At the beginning of the second year, the landlord must return to the tenant any amount that exceeds the amount of one month's rent.

206. (2) A lease for a term of more than three years must be written in order to be enforceable. In Pennsylvania, leases may be written, oral, or implied. The statute of frauds in Pennsylvania applies to leases for more than three years' duration. An oral lease for three years or less is usually enforceable.

207. (2) In addition to regularly scheduled meetings, the Commission holds public meetings to solicit from members of the public suggestions, comments, and objections about real estate practice in this commonwealth (202(e)).

208. (1) Continuing education is required of individuals holding either a broker's or salesperson's license. The requirement does not apply to cemetery brokers, cemetery salespeople, builder-owner salespersons, time-share salespeople, campground membership salespeople, or rental listing referral agents (35.382).

209. (4) An advertisement that offers prizes, certificates, or gifts must contain the fair market value of each prize, certificate, or gift; a description of each prize, certificate, or gift; and the odds of winning each prize, certificate, or gift (35.306).

210. (3) Rules of the Commission do not dictate which broker must retain an earnest money deposit in an escrow account. Either the listing or selling broker may hold the deposit with proper notification to the buyer and seller (35.323).

211. (1) A licensee must notify the Commission of being convicted of, or pleading guilty or *nolo contendere* to, a felony or misdemeanor within 30 days of the verdict or plea. The notification requirement applies to any conviction, regardless of the offense involved (35.290).

212. (2) The Commission will not authorize relicensure of an individual whose license has been revoked for at least five years. If relicensure is permitted, the individual must comply with current requirements for licensure before the license is issued (35.251).

213. (1) A licensee who provides insurance, construction, repair, or inspection services that are utilized by the consumer must provide the consumer a written disclosure of the financial interest (including a referral fee or commission) that the licensee has in the service. The disclosure must be made when the licensee first advises the consumer that the service is available or when the licensee first learns that the consumer will be utilizing the service (35.283). In certain circumstances, a licensee may accept fees paid directly to the licensee.

214. (4) The purpose and goals of continuing education are to provide education through which licensees can maintain and increase competency; keep abreast of changes in laws, regulations, practices, and procedures; and ensure that the public is protected. Generation of revenue to the Commission is not a goal of mandatory continuing education (35.381).

215. (3) A transaction licensee owes the duty of limited confidentiality and may not disclose to a buyer that the seller will accept a price less than the asking/listing price of the property (35.316). Providing assistance with document preparation, advising the consumer about compliance with laws pertaining to transactions, and keeping the consumer informed about tasks to be completed are all general duties of all licensees (35.292).

216. (3) Rental payments may not be deposited in the broker's escrow account (35.321(b)). The escrow account must be maintained in a federally or state-insured bank or recognized depository, must designate the broker as trustee, and must provide for withdrawal of funds without prior notice (35.325).

217. (1) In the event the Pennsylvania Human Relations Commission does not act on a discrimination complaint within 90 days after it is filed with the Pennsylvania Human Relations Commission, then the state Real Estate Commission may proceed with action against the licensee. The 90-day waiting period applies only in initial complaints against the licensee (604(22)).

218. (2) A person acting as trustee in bankruptcy, administrator, executor, trustee, or guardian while acting under court order or under the authority of a will or trust instrument is not required to hold a real estate license (304(5)).

219. (4) All fees required under the Real Estate Licensing and Registration Act are fixed by the Real Estate Commission by regulation (407).

220. (1) Licenses will be granted only to, and renewed only for, persons who bear a good reputation for honesty, trustworthiness, integrity, and competence to transact business (501). Citizenship is not required for licensure. A candidate must disclose details of convictions, but the disclosure does not preclude the possibility of licensure. Financial solvency is not required as a condition of licensure.

221. (2) Whenever a licensed salesperson or associate broker desires to change his or her employment from one licensed broker to another, the salesperson must notify the Commission in writing no later than ten days after the intended date of change, pay the required fee, and return the current license (603(a)).

222. (2) Unless otherwise agreed, a licensee owes no duty to conduct an independent inspection of the property and owes no duty to independently verify the accuracy or completeness of any representation made by a consumer to a transaction reasonably believed by the licensee to be accurate and reliable (606.1(i)).

223. (3) The employing broker designated as trustee may give a licensed employee written authority to withdraw funds from the escrow account for payments that are properly chargeable to the account (35.325).

224. (4) Written agreements between brokers and consumers that obligate a consumer to pay a fee, commission, or other valuable consideration must contain information as required by section 608.3 of the Real Estate Licensing and Registration Act. A broker, with the written consent of the principal, may designate a licensee to act exclusively as an agent of the seller/landlord and another licensee to act exclusively as an agent of the buyer/tenant in the case where a broker serves as a dual agent (35.315).

225. (4) A comparative market analysis may be prepared by a contracted buyer's agent for the purpose of determining the offering price for a specified piece of real estate in an identified real estate market at a specified time (201).